Alien... Arab... and maybe
Illegal in America

To order additional copies, please contact us.
BookSurge, LLC
www.booksurge.com
1-866-308-6235
orders@booksurge.com

MOHAMED FANDI

ALIEN... ARAB... AND MAYBE ILLEGAL IN AMERICA

Special Edition

BookSurge Publishing
2006

Alien... Arab... and maybe
Illegal in America

Alien...Arab...and Maybe Illegal in America by Mohamed Fandi as reviewed by New York Times best selling author Ellen Tanner Marsh

Mohamed Fandi's *Alien...Arab...and Maybe Illegal in America* begins as a compelling study of why millions of illegal aliens are willing to risk everything to live in America, particularly after the tragedies of September 11, 2001. What we soon understand, however, is that this book is an often chilling account of what it means to be an Arab—even more, a Muslim—in a country where tolerance has been stretched to the breaking point...and often beyond.

With more than twelve million illegal aliens residing in the United States, the public is inundated with news features about political wrangling over immigration laws and the ongoing controversy about border patrols. In *Alien...Arab...and Maybe Illegal in America*, U.S. citizen Mohamed Fandi presents an insider's view into a world of which little is written, except in the most volatile and sometimes offensive manner: the Arab alien.

In a methodical and highly logical fashion, Fandi offers the clearest rationale given to date about what motivates perhaps hundreds of thousands of Arab Muslims to overstay a visa and risk deportation. He also explains why so many of these people choose to remain in a country where anti-Arab sentiment is running higher than at anytime in our history. Between the overt racism and the fear generated by the Patriots Act, one is hard-pressed to understand the willingness to be subjected to arrest, abuse, and public denunciation. Thanks to Mohamed Fandi's clear guidance, much of this confusion is now resolved.

PRAISE FOR Mohamed Fandi´s Alien...Arab...and Maybe Illegal in America

"There are more than twelve million illegal aliens residing in the United States... A Fascinating Look into Why Illegal Aliens are Willing to Risk it All to Live in America"

BookSurge LLC, An Amazon.com company.

"The United States has seen a large influx of immigrants over the past few decades... Mohamed Fandi writes a fascinating account of what it means to be a foreigner and an Arab living day-to-day in America, particularly after September 11... Fandi answers some important questions: Why would an Arab choose to overstay his visa and risk deportation? And why he prefers to live here, with all of the concomitant post-9/11 racism, when he could remain in, or return to, his native country and live in peace? What is most compelling, however, is the view offered into the mind and heart of U.S.-based Arabs, and particularly Muslims. How did these proud people feel, being painted with one large brushstroke as terrorists? How did they manage, day to day, to work, send their children to school...live their lives?"

BookSurge LLC, An Amazon.com company.

"In a methodical and highly logical fashion, Fandi offers the clearest rationale given to date about what motivates perhaps hundreds of thousands of Arab Muslims to overstay a visa and risk deportation..."

New York Times best selling author.

I Only Dedicate This Book To People I Don't Know…
And Particularly To Those Immigrants Who Choose To
Live In The Other Side Of Their Legitimate Frontiers.

CONTENTS

PREFACE xv

Chapter 1 : *Significant Historic Dates*
    Affecting U.S. Immigration
    (and the rest of the world) 1

Chapter 2 : *Nostalgia* 7

Chapter 3 : *The Quest for Light* 13

Chapter 4 : *Stimulus to Escape the Country* 19

Chapter 5 : *The making of Decision to come to US* 23

Chapter 6 : *Welcome to America* 31

Chapter 7 : *"Los Papeles" ... How, and why?* 35

Chapter 8 : *The Start of a new Life* 39

Chapter 9 : *What's coming?* 43

Chapter 10 : *5 years in America because of my ID* 47

Chapter 11 : *Two out of three Goals* 53

Chapter 12 : *No Time for Love.* 59

Chapter 13 : *Do you speak English?* 63

Chapter 14 : *Kiss the Green Card* 69

Chapter 15 : *A year in America: no worries* 75

Chapter 16 : *More years, more worries -in America-* . . 79

Chapter 17 : *Next step: bye America* 87

EPILOGUE 93

PREFACE

Today's immigrants come from all parts of the world. The current phase of immigration history followed the elimination of strict quotas based on nationality. In 1978, the U.S. government set an annual world-wide quota of 290,000. This ceiling was raised again in 1990 to 700,000. Immigrants have arrived at a rate that at times has exceeded 1,000,000 new arrivals per year. These new arrivals have settled in all parts of the country. America is a nation of immigrants! We are all sons and daughters of immigrants and the cultural diversity of America has served to enrich and strengthen the nation. The greatness of America is a reflection of the sacrifice, contributions and efforts of immigrants. They have greatly enriched the history of the United States. There is reason to celebrate the richness of the cultural diversity that immigration has brought to America!

An "immigrant," according to the United States definition, refers to any alien admitted to the United States as a lawful permanent resident. Permanent residents are also commonly referred to as immigrants; however, the Immigration and Nationality Act (INA) broadly defines an immigrant as any alien in the United States, except one legally admitted under specific nonimmigrant categories. An illegal alien who entered the United States without inspection, for example, would be technically classified as an immigrant under the INA but is not a permanent resident alien. Lawful permanent residents are legally accorded the privilege of residing permanently in the United States. They may be issued immigrant visas by the Department of State overseas or adjusted to permanent resident status by the Immigration and Naturalization Service in the United States.

However, an alien who seeks temporary entry to the United States for a specific purpose is considered a non-immigrant. This type of alien must have a permanent residence abroad (for most classes of admission) and qualify for the nonimmigrant classification sought. The nonimmigrant classifications include: foreign government officials, visitors for business and for pleasure, aliens in transit through the United States, treaty traders and investors, students, international representatives, *temporary workers and trainees,* representatives of foreign information media, exchange visitors, fiancé(e)s of U.S. citizens, intra-company transferees, NATO officials, religious workers, and some others. Most nonimmigrants can be accompanied or joined by spouses and unmarried minor (or dependent) children.

As the events of 2001-2003 unfolded, prompting revised and new laws related to the immigration and homeland security, I began to feel an obligation to write what I experienced as a foreigner, alien and Arab in America for my fellow immigrants from all over the world and to the American citizens to discover how the would-be life to be of an illegal to live in U.S. However, this book is a first-person account, not an academic history. The book, therefore, tells what one immigrant saw, thought, experienced, lived, and believed from one perspective. Others who were involved in the same events will, no doubt, recall them differently. I do not say they have better experiences or worse ones, only that this account is what I believe I experienced. I want to apologize in advance to the reader for the frequent use of the first-person singular, but I found it was impossible to avoid as I related my story.

The "story" is necessarily incomplete. Many key events and people are not mentioned, while others who deserve rich description are only briefly introduced. I have tried, wherever possible, to respect the privacy and confidences of those about whom I write, including myself. I recognize there is a great risk in writing a book such as this and that I might be in some kind of trouble with the federal authorities regarding the illegal presence of an immigrant in U.S.

Some will say this book is a proof of apology, a request for a better life. It is meant to be factual and sometimes polemical. I have spent a decade living the Immigrant-Alien-Arab life, with all the fluctuations after the 9/11 attacks and other attacks around the world linked to some Islamic groups. As a result of the combination of being an Alien and an Arab, a person in all circumstances might be automatically assumed to be an Illegal, thus the title, "Alien … Arab… and maybe illegal in America." Many important steps were also taken in that decade as the result of the sacrifice of thousands of Immigrants, those who serve the country of USA. Where I couldn't get any advantage by my presence in U.S., I have tried to be fair in recounting what I know from either my life in the States or my Arab race. I leave bottom-line evaluations of supports and disagreements to the reader.

CHAPTER 1
Significant Historic Dates Affecting U.S. Immigration (and the Rest of the World)

Naturalization Act of 1790 Stipulated that "any alien, being a free white person, may be admitted to become a citizen of the United States."

1875 Supreme Court declared that regulation of immigration is the responsibility of the Federal Government.

1882 **The Chinese Exclusion Act** prohibited certain laborers from immigrating to the United States.

1885 **and** 1887 Alien Contract Labor laws which prohibited certain laborers from immigrating to the United States.

1891 The Federal Government assumed the task of inspecting, admitting, rejecting, and processing all immigrants seeking admission to the U.S.

1892 On January 2, a new Federal immigration station opened on Ellis Island in New York Harbor.

1903 This Act restated the 1891 provisions concerning land borders and called for rules covering entry as well as inspection of aliens crossing the Mexican border.

1907 **The Immigration Act of** 1907 reorganized the states bordering Mexico (Arizona, New Mexico and a large part of Texas) into Mexican Border District to stem the flow of immigrants into the U.S.

1917—1924 A series of laws were enacted to further

limit the number of new immigrants. These laws established the quota system and imposed passport requirements. They expanded the categories of excludable aliens and banned all Asians except Japanese.

1924 **Act** Reduced the number of immigration visas and allocated them on the basis of national origin.

1940 **The Alien Registration Act** required all aliens (non-U.S. citizens) within the United States to register with the Government and receive an Alien Registration Receipt Card (the predecessor of the "green card").

1950 **Passage of the Internal Security Act** which rendered the Alien Registration Receipt Card even more valuable. Immigrants with legal status had their cards replaced with what generally became known as the "green card" (Form I-151).

1952 **Act** Established the modern day immigration system. It created a quota system which imposes limits on a per-country basis. It also established the preference system that gave priority to family members and people with special skills.

1968 **Act** Eliminated immigration discrimination based on race, place of birth, sex and residence. It also officially abolished restrictions on Oriental immigration.

1976 **Act** Eliminated preferential treatment for residents of the Western Hemisphere.

1980 **Act** Established a general policy governing the admission of refugees.

1986 **Act** Focused on curtailing illegal immigration. It legalized hundred of thousands of illegal immigrants. It also introduced the employer sanctions program which fines employers for hiring illegal workers. It also passed tough laws to prevent bogus marriage fraud.

1990 Act Established an annual limit for certain categories of immigrants. It was aimed at helping U.S. businesses attract skilled foreign workers; thus, it expanded the business class categories to favor persons who can make educational, professional or financial contributions. It created the Immigrant Investor Program.

USA Patriot Act 2001: Uniting and Strengthening America by providing appropriate tools required to intercept and obstruct terrorism.

Creation of the USCIS 2003: As of March 1, 2003, the Immigration and Naturalization Service becomes part of the Department of Homeland Security (DHS). The department's new U.S. Citizenship and Immigration Services (USCIS) function is to handle immigration services and benefits, including citizenship, applications for permanent residence, non-immigrant applications, asylum, and refugee services. Immigration enforcement functions are now under the Department's Border and Transportation Security Directorate, known as the Bureau of Immigration and Customs Enforcement (BICE).

After this succinct presentation of significant immigration dates, it would be unconceivable to exclude the intrinsic beauty of American immigration today that allows freedom and opportunity to all. U.S. immigration policy does not discriminate based on race, religion, creed and color.

The statistics of the illegal alien resident population in 1996 which was updated in December of 2001 shows that about 5 million undocumented immigrants were residing in the United States in October 1996, with a range of about 4.6 to 5.4 million. The population was estimated to be growing by about 275,000 each year, which is about 25,000 lower than the annual level of growth estimated by the INS in 1994.

California is the leading state of residence with 2 million, or 40 percent of the undocumented population. The 7 states with the largest estimated numbers of undocumented immigrants are California (2.0 million), Texas (700,000), New York (540,000), Florida (350,000), Illinois (290,000), New Jersey (135,000), and Arizona (115,000). These states accounted for 83 percent of the total immigrant population in October of 1996.

The 5.0 million undocumented immigrants made up about 1.9 percent of the total U.S. population, with the highest percentages in California, the District of Columbia, and Texas. In the majority of states, undocumented residents comprise less than 1 percent of the population.

Mexico is the leading country of origin with 2.7 million, or 54 percent of the population. The Mexican undocumented population has grown at an average annual rate of just over 150,000 since 1988. The 14 countries with 50,000 or more undocumented immigrants in 1996 accounted for 81 percent of the total population. The large majority, over 80 percent, of all undocumented immigrants are from countries in the Western Hemisphere.

About 2.1 million, or 41 percent, of the total undocumented population in 1996 are nonimmigrant overstays. That is, they entered legally on a temporary basis and failed to depart. The proportion of the undocumented population who are overstays varies considerably by country of origin. About 16 percent of the Mexican undocumented population consists of non-immigrant overstays, compared to 26 percent of those from Central America, and 91 percent from all other countries.

Coming to the USA and starting a new life in the United States like many settlers did 250 years ago was my biggest dream. It all started with a dream, an aspiration, a need to change my life, and a leap of faith. A day or two after I land on U.S. ground reality strikes and things need to be done!

What was my goal? Visitor Tourist Visa (B2), Visitor Business Visa (B1), US Student Visa (F1), Exchange Visitor (J1) Fiancée Visa (K1), Green Card through Employment, Green Card through Marriage, Family Relations, Temporary Professionals (H1B), Religious Worker, Temporary Religious Worker, Political Asylum or Citizenship?

CHAPTER 2
Nostalgia

I remember...I was getting off the plane; I didn't have a clear idea of what was going to happen. I didn't know what I was going to do. I didn't know how to communicate, how to persuade, how to give, how to obtain or how to win. I just knew that it was going to be better and I was sure; then again maybe I wasn't...Can you imagine yourself starting your life from the beginning? All you know is in the past and it is not going to exist anymore?

I remember...I wanted to be someone; I wanted to become somebody very useful, very important in society, someone who would go back to his country with all the knowledge needed to achieve my dreams, dreams that all the country still hope to accomplish.

I remember watching myself with pride, looking in the mirror as someone different. I looked at my family's eyes and faces with courage. They were very proud and happy for me; they were really satisfied. They didn't ask when I was coming back. They were content in knowledge I was reaching for my dream. They knew I needed to accomplish this dream before we could discuss the date of my return.

I remember I didn't really have an absolute plan and desire to come to America. I didn't envisage it. I didn't –maybe- believe in it.

I wanted to have the seat by the window in the plane so I could see and say 'good-bye' to my country. Unfortunately the only seat I could get was in the middle of the row, but I remember I felt I was looking through the glass, and I said 'bye, and thank you my country.'

I looked back to say 'bye' to my family, to keep the sight always in my mind. I looked back to memorize every part of the situation. I looked back to have more tenacity, to obtain more faith, and to gain more strength and determination to accomplish my dream.

I took the plane and exited scared, confused and happy. I was going somewhere else; I was flying and leaving everything behind me. I knew that my family was still there, I was just with them thirty minutes ago. Yet I also knew I wasn't going to see them for at least thirty months. I didn't want to think about it, I didn't want to count on it. Believe it or not; it didn't make a difference.

I wasn't sure there was a reason for me to go back or come here. All my beliefs, convictions and thoughts lead me to one conclusion: never let a chance and opportunity pass you by or fade away; there is only one destiny, one chance. You take it or you let it go. If you leave it there is no other.

I didn't think or plan to come here. I didn't know what to do. I wouldn't hope that something so good could happen to me. I didn't want to speak about it; it's weak (from my point of view) to decide to leave your country, it's similar to failing and it is a defect.

It was my fault: I shouldn't leave and I shouldn't let it go. I was wrong, I was stupid, maybe I wasn't ready; it was planned to be the last year of my studies, and because I didn't succeed to pass one of the last exams in the Law University I thought that everything was finished for me, there was no future for me. I know by now that I was wrong, but back then I only saw that I didn't succeed. I let my chance go away, pass by. I didn't have any more choices (or another chance). Everyone was against me, and I didn't blame anyone. I needed another start. I needed to commence everything from the beginning. I had no choice. That was my only option. No game, no game anymore. There is a need of another chance, but where is it? How can I get it?

I was still in the university (college here). After I got my baccalaureate, which is similar to high school. I then went to the university to study the law, mostly in French. I was so happy and proud of myself. My friends and my parents were so proud of me. I had my own privacy and I did whatever I wanted. None of my relatives were worried about my future. In the high school, all the students are the same; there are no differences between any of us. There was no rich or poor. We were all just friends even though we didn't know each other's lives. It took a few years to get to college (university), and I still had not faced any complex choices. Everyone was confident with all my decisions.

In the high school everything was nice. She was there. For me, she is still and always there. Maybe when I come back, she will be still there. I think about her; I keep always thinking about her. I don't know if we are going to meet again. She was the flower of my childhood. She used to have black hair and hazel eyes. She was not short but not too tall with a beautiful smile, but most important she was absolutely very kind, her name was Soraya. But, there was that other boy with her all the time. He got a car and I didn't. They were saying that he got the papers of Italy in French language. We used to call those kinds of people 'les vacanciers' or 'the tourists'. They go to work abroad and, after just two or three months of being

9

outside of their country, they came back with different cars, more money and other benefits the occidental lifestyle can give. They began to look different and started to act differently than the local people. They got more confident and satisfied and they were happier than before, different than when they were living in their native country of origin. Above all, they could get whatever they wanted; For instance, having girls to go out with is one of the most essential advantages their trips to Europe provide them. The same scenario is observed among the South American societies (Mexicans for example). When they come to the United States of America and spend some years in the States, they go back to their origin countries acting differently, showing the local residents all kind of contradictions and dissimilarities that help to break down all the native and domestic beliefs and habits and making them (local inhabitants) feel guilty of something they never had done. However they would also like to learn those 'values' by immigrating to the United States of America.

Before I came to USA a close friend of Soraya told me that she was pregnant, and I even heard she got married to the same guy 'from' Italy. We never went for a date, but I always loved her and I think she loved me too. Our routes were different, and they would never cross again...

I also remember I was 7 years old. I was devoted learning as much as I could from every day's lesson. I had many idols to learn from and imitate: my parents, my grandparents, the teachers at school, soccer players, the elder people (actually there is always a magnificent respect for older people in our society), even the heroes in some books like Ali-Baba, Sinbad, and others performing in the cartoons on television.

It was a day just like any other regular one. I woke up exactly at 7.00 am and I went straight ahead to the bathroom. I washed my face, hands, my mouth and my eyes. Then I walked toward the living room. It was still dark; it was a winter day and I could barely see the light through the windows, but there was a small tiny light coming in from the window. My grandparents were already awake. At that age, I always thought they were the first and the only people 'in the world' to wake up that early.

My grandfather, with a nice and pure smile, sat with my hot soup ready for me. He always adds some olive oil and cumin. He used to say they were healthier than anything else during that time of the day. I can still remember the smell of the food. My grandmother –always wearing a traditional dress– was usually the first of the whole family to wake up in the 'big' house. She was short, between white and brown skin color, with very black dark hair. She always had something to say or to remark. She served us tea, a light tea, not too strong, the perfect drink to start a nice and smooth day. Anytime during the day you go to our 'big' house, my grandmother will serve you tea; it doesn't matter if you are a guest or a member of the family who lives there.

"Good morning", said my grandma.

"Good morning grandma, good morning grandpa".

My grandpa smiled and said "good morning".

"Where is your brother?" my grandma asked, "Is he still in the bed?"

"No, he is in the bedroom." I replied.

"Go call him. Tell him to hurry up. It's almost time for school. The bus will be here at anytime now," my grandma said.

"Okay," I answered.

Before I went looking for him, he was coming through

the door. "Here I am grandma, good morning," my brother said.

On the table, there was hot tea with herbal mint, homemade bread, olive oil, a plate with a mix of honey and butter ghee, some almonds, pecans, butter and jam. While we were eating, my grandma brought two bowls of durum wheat soup, one for her and the other for my grandpa.

After we finished eating, my grandmother opened the window. There was a nice breeze coming from outside. She opened the window so we could hear the horn of the bus when it came. My grandfather start singing for my brother and me a song that we got familiar with. The song was about those who have a better life (he called it gold) and win many opportunities just by waking up early in the morning compared to those who wake up late and miss all they could take advantage of. He was still singing; he was singing for a new day, singing for his memories, and singing because he was happy. He knew there was nothing better than sitting and having breakfast with his family.

In our family, people live for a long time. My grandmother has an uncle who lives in the south of my country. He is still alive, and in a good health. We used to, and still do, call him "the engineer" because he knows about everything (except how people could get to the moon; it was over his mind's capacity to accept it). He has been living all his life in the countryside. He has two houses, and two bikes; we always rode the bikes together and sometimes we even raced each other. The bike was the main method of transportation in the city. Whenever we were going to the south with my family, we always stayed with him in one of his houses. He is a happy, enthusiastic and very energetic person. He had been living four generations, and he has seen five or six kings succeeding each other.

CHAPTER 3
The Quest for Light

Thank you for choosing the Royal Moroccan Airlines Company. We hope you enjoyed your trip and look forward serving you in the future, thank you." That was it, that's it. It was the last service, the last product, the last donation, and the last 'direct' contact with my country.

I was already in the United States of America; did I ever make it that far before? I felt like a butterfly opening its wings for the first time toward the light, fresh and ready. I never made it that far. It was a strange feeling.

What is going to be my 'first' awareness, my first impression? What will be the first service I'm going to receive from the Americans, the initial product, the foremost donation and the primary contact? Is this 'great satisfaction' going to last for a while or forever? I didn't know. I doubted it.

I'm in the land of freedom, the land of business, the land where every day many people around the country become rich, millionaires and on the other side many become or are very poor. You lose or you win, you succeed or you fail, you convert to someone important or you stay who you are; this is America, it's about a dream becoming reality.

It was nothing like what I expected, no donation, no contact, and no product, nothing at all but freedom. You do whatever you want to do, stay, go, move, sing, scream, or sleep. No one cares about you. You have your own space, and it is all yours, nobody can mess with it. Either you alone or with millions of people there is no difference, and it is a world of opportunities for an immigrant who needs all kind of privacies to distinguish himself as a winner among all other nationalities. An immigrant is somebody who left the package of a lifestyle behind him to adapt himself to new customs. Nevertheless, traditions and customs in the United States of America have been originally developed to respect all people's backgrounds.

I passed through the immigration office (Immigration and Naturalization Services) so they could check out my passport and visa, and it was the easiest door I ever moved through. It was even much easier than going by the main door of the middle school when I came late for school in the presence of the security guy.

'Thumbs up.' My English wasn't that good, but my presence was enough; my appearance was talking for me. There was no major search of my things. I got my luggage, and I went out from the airport, JFK airport.

What I felt? It is absolutely amazing. I just experienced exactly the same feeling I have now: the sensation to explore more freedom and that is the biggest advantage about living in America. It is actually not only freedom by itself as a result, but it also concerns the way people accomplish, fight and establish that freedom. A history of many fluctuations drove the country into self respect of values and people's dignity, whichever is your nationality.

The level of immigration in this country is the highest in the world. U.S.A is a big and spacious country and Uncle Sam always needs people from all over the world to work and spend their lives or a part of it in this land. I was not an exception; I had the chance to come to America. Moreover, I think that more than half of my country (and each country around the world) would be ready —anytime- to visit or stay in the States. No one can predict the future, but as long as America is the first and biggest 'economy' in the world, every human being expresses a wish to live the American 'dream.' Coming for business, for studying, for entertainment or for any other reason are only excuses and 'explanations' just to stay in U.S.A.

However, nobody could ignore how hard it is for any immigrant to obtain the right to get into the American soil. I still remember few years ago, back home, the line of people waiting next to the U.S embassy was so long. It was 6.55 am and it was really hot. The security policemen were trying to make order in the line. People might have to spend the night in the street. Some of them do that regularly and every day till they could get their appointment. The line was moving slowly. Although I was in the line, I didn't feel it move. We were waiting for the line to move faster, which it didn't, and our patience and endurance fade as we wait to get inside. Actually, it moved but it was hard to concentrate, hard to think between two choices; to get the visa at the embassy is on one side, but its not that easy to get to it and you don't know what it is going to happen, and on the other side go back to the real life with all the routine and nothing to sacrifice or lose. In the second option you leave the line and look for another line, if there is another one.

The U.S. embassy is one of many other embassies where you might buy a spot in the 'line.' It's a business matter in the French, the Belgium, the Italian or other European countries... the same situation; people spend nights there. Their purpose is not to obtain visas, but they are there spending time and long nights in the street next to the embassy doors and windows; they are there to 'sell' their spots in the coming morning to people trying to apply for papers or visas. They sell them the closest spots to the doors of the embassies.

I was there waiting for my turn, the total hour, the whole morning, the entire day. I was lucky that was a day before a holiday, because they gave tickets for appointments for everyone. My rendezvous was in two weeks.

Nowadays, the situation is worse for people to get an appointment; it is around two months or more. And it is more or less the case in every country around the world.

In Kenya, for instance, to schedule an appointment with the US embassy, there used to be just one phone line in the whole country. Every Kenyan citizen had to use the same phone number to call and everyone called the same phone. The whole country didn't have choice but one number. Obviously, it is busy all the time. A Kenyan friend of mine told me his story; he said that he had to wait between four and five months to get someone on the other side of the line. He was lucky that early morning because at the end the phone was ringing. He got it; no one was calling that time from anywhere in Kenya. When was his appointment? In two months, that was the answer. So, our Kenyan friend had to spend six months or half a year just to have his appointment ready, just to talk to someone, just to talk with a visa official, just to let them know he wanted to come to America. And maybe, he will get the visa maybe he will not get it, but for sure, he will become a celebrity in his Kenyan neighborhood; his parents, his friends and his family will be proud and happy for him. Is he going to come back to Kenya in case they let him go to the USA? I don't think so.

It is going to be a huge decision for a Kenyan, a Mexican, and a Moroccan or even for a French immigrant to go back. It has never been easy for an alien to make up his or her mind, to leave America behind with no paper to assure the return. No one wants to risk it. Nobody wants to lose the 'power' of being in the United States of America.

CHAPTER 4
Stimulus to Escape the Country

We love our origins, our races. Why did I leave my country? I never thought about living abroad. I didn't want to come, neither that Mexican nor that Polish wanted to.

We didn't dream about it when we were kids. We are proud of our heritage in our countries, of our people, our language, of our land, of our backgrounds, of ourselves. It was an obligation, absolutely a sacrifice, a choice, a decision to move to the United States of America.

I remember I was in my third year in the university; if I failed there was no other possibility but the door, the street... why? I didn't need to know why. I didn't have time to spend to answer this question. I needed to move on.

I couldn't risk losing, not anymore. I was already 22 years old; I remembered being a nice guy. My field was the study of the law, the law in French language; that's what I studied in the university. I was going to become a lawyer, a manager of the Juridical Department in a private company, a bank or even an international advocate.

I know the law. I never wanted to do something to break the rules; any rules that have been made by the authorities are supposed to be respected. I'm not an American, but I live in America. Therefore I am supposed to adhere to their regulations. If my visa expires, I obviously need to leave the country. That's the law, it says so. We all know that, but am I really ready to be aware of it? Do I care about the consequences? Am I really interested in respecting this law? Is it really fair to apply it for my situation? What is the difference between an American person and me? Are we both human beings? Couldn't he go to my country without any need for a visa? Does he need to wait six month to see an employee of the immigration in his country? Don't –for instance- Mexicans have the right to live and explore another country? Don't foreigners have the right to visit or stay in the States, the freedom of circulation in the earth? We are all human beings, and the world -as far as I know- belongs to everyone, to the humans and beings (nature, animals, plants, people…) with no restrictions I think. This is just a theory although the consulate, the embassy, the governments or the I.N.S don't really bother themselves to worry about all that.

There are some opportunities in Morocco, but there was no chance for me, not for going back and starting over. I didn't want to try again. I didn't think it was a smart idea to spend more than seven years studying and then 'gambling' for my future; maybe I work, maybe I stay home.

Nevertheless, I didn't pass the third year in the university; I got the chance to switch into other courses, which led me – with a big coincidence and luck of course- to watch 'super bowl football.' Now I don't blame my failure. It guided me to be in the United States and building a routine that let me take the 'blue line' subway in Chicago everyday to go to work. Without my failure, I wouldn't be in the USA. I wouldn't have a credit card on my key chain. By that time in 1999, one year before the 21st century, to open a bank account in Morocco, you needed a job, a justification for working delivery from the company you work for, a justification for a good income, an interview and many other documents, plus an investigation to complete the process of obtaining a checkbook, not even a credit card!!! For a credit card it would be a worse story. Many examples justify the huge difference between societies.

A big part of our happiness and pride to be in this country emanates from our relatives and parents attitudes. Those people made us 'heroes' just by being in the USA. A big percentage of the foreign communities stay here just because they want to keep that value and statue (the privilege of being in America) going on and alive. They would rather go back home, but it is better for them to hide making their relatives proud of them and not break their dreams. They do not want to wake up; their availability is managed by the need of a better life.

They stay in America, work, work, and work like "burros." They work for the American dream, work for the others. They work to pay their bills, to feed the stress. They work for minimum wage, they work to make more money, they work to live better, and they work of course to be a part of the system. The system needs them. The system needs you. It is proud of you, but the system won't sacrifice itself for anyone. You have to give up yourself for it, for the nation, for USA, for George W. Bush!!! We are mad.

I didn't pass. That's why I'm here. I left the exam, I smoked a Marlboro cigarette, and I was thinking what's next? Next is: Nothing, nada, rien.

I took a deep breath; it came...a private school, which was it. But, they are expensive, my family can't afford it...we didn't even mention or talk about it. I knew it was out of question. At the end there was no other option than that one.

What do I usually like? What do I enjoy? What time of the year do I enjoy more? It was the summer; I liked it more especially when I was at school. Why? It is because most of the people are not working throughout the summer. It is the holiday, the sun, the beaches…moreover I would like to enjoy more time during that period of the year, to have more fun despite of my job. What is going to be then the field I can enjoy more? What will it be? It is going to be the Tourism, Travel Industry, Leisure, entertainment…that's what I'm going to study. As a result, those studies showed me the way to end my courses in USA as a new experience and different type of tourism skills.

Events led to others, and by the close link related the 'tourism, hotel management' to the restaurant business. I didn't find it hard to find jobs in hotels or restaurants. However the majority of foreigners in USA work in the Food and Beverage profession; from dishwashers to chefs in the kitchen, and from busboy or food runner, to manager or supervisor in the 'front door.'

CHAPTER 5
The Making of the Decision to Come to the US

I graduated as the 'first' student in my promotion. Two years in a private school were a challenge with a mosaic of courses, a different level of competition, and more open ways and methods to learn than the public way. It was much more simple and easier than the university. The simple and easy way conducted me to America; the free way took me to the free country. If I stayed in the university I wouldn't be able to watch the 'Jimmy Kimmel Live' show.

Before I got my 'Tourism & Hotel Management' diploma, we had a visit at school from Mr. "Saver." He was a Moroccan-American citizen, in his 40s or 50s. He came to our school— among other schools all over the country- as an ambassador of a partnership program with the American Academy. The Academy hired him and sent him to go to different countries and choose students to come over to America in order to accomplish an exchange program in various areas: Florida, South Carolina or other states.

First, I didn't believe that Mr. 'Saver' was going to take us to the USA. It sounded easy and possible for anyone; there were no extra conditions but the ability to speak some English, TOEFL with a minimum of 450 points and paying a fee of about a thousand dollars for the internship. That money will pay for our housing, transportation to and from work and other facilities and social events are also included for the whole year.

At school, I was the weakest in English. But for the possibility and the chance of coming to the USA, I had to do more than my best; I needed to give it a shot. Two of my friends succeeded. They passed the test, and they were already in America. I got to do it too; I had to get the TOEFL. The first time, I failed with a score of 367, but did I give up? No. This was the only time I had a second chance. I went the second time to another city, the capital of Morocco to have the test. The second time was good, my TOEFL score was 450 points even, just what I needed, the exact total to let me have another fate and luck in the future.

Mr. 'Saver' told us to go, me and some other students, to the embassy. He said he had already talked to them and they will give us the visa. So, about two weeks later I went to the interview. I was well dressed and shaved with a cravat, a nice jacket, and some perfume...I was waiting for about three hours, which made my appearance change. It felt like forever to get my turn; I wasn't the only one there. Many of us with the same program were waiting for the 'shiny' day, for the visa to be stamped on their passports.

I heard my number over the speakers. I got up; everyone was staring at me. I heard before that on this day it would be rare for someone to obtain a visa. Some interviewees were circulating that it was an unlucky day. I never believed in superstition, and I had to try my chance anyways. There were four windows for the candidates; in each one of them there is an immigration officer who speaks a different language than the others: English, French or Arabic. The first language they asked you if you could speak is English. If you couldn't speak English they then asked you about French or Moroccan. Moreover, there is more chance to get a visa if you speak fluent English than someone who doesn't.

The officer asked me which language I would prefer and I said it doesn't matter any of them. I can speak all of them. The truth was that I couldn't speak English. At the end, I didn't say that to them. I was coming to the USA for learning, for courses, and my English was supposed to be good. So we started in English, and obviously we finished our discussion in French. He started with the question about the reasons I wanted to go to the States and then if I had any proof about the school I was going to or the courses I was going to take. Mr. 'Saver' didn't tell them anything. Actually it was stupid of me and that was the problem. I didn't have yet the contract or the papers to justify the contract gathering the Academy and me; they call it 166, the pink form. The officer asked for it and I told him that someone (Saver) was supposed to call the Embassy. What the hell? I told him that he might call your office. Then he went to check and he came back giving me back my documents; he declined the visa. I was losing the game before even starting it. I didn't have anything with me to apply but the passport, some small pictures and 45 dollars —that was the fee for the application. There was no way to get the visa that day. He returned my passport; I needed to return here in two months to reapply.

Where was he? Where was 'our saver'? He was staying in the Hyatt Regency hotel in Casablanca, a nice, luxurious four-star hotel. I called the front desk; I asked for him and they said he wasn't there. I went to the hotel; I called his room from the lobby. At the end, he was coming from outside drunk. He said he needed to go to his room, and he will meet us downstairs in the café in 10 to 15 minutes. We waited for more than 30 minutes and he still didn't show up. 45 minutes later, he finally showed up and he seemed to be busy. He said he didn't have enough time. He asked everyone what happened and asked each of us about the interview individually. There were eight of us that had been declined the visas, and we all failed the interview with the consulate. He told us to just relax, and that everything will be ok. He ordered us to leave now, go home, and he will contact us. He said he would meet with some informed and important people in the Governmental Office of the Tourism. He added that he was going to do all the possible maneuvers to get us the visa. There is no other choice but trust to what he was saying. I went home with no hope. I was disappointed but determined to do something.

My father at home told me to invite the 'saver' for lunch one day before he went to the USA again. He accepted the invitation. He was happy to meet with my parents. That day my father picked him from the hotel. My mother cooked the traditional Moroccan food, 'the Couscous.' We all were there, my whole family, including me there were my two brothers and my parents. We had lunch all together and we talked about anything. Mr. 'Saver' said to my father that they would be proud of me in the future once I went to the USA, and my parents liked him. He usually talks too much, but with my father I felt they were in the same level. Actually they were more or less the same age. He also told my father we were going to have a better life and a better house than the one we have now. My father asked him about the chances I had to get the visa. He assured him that he would do all he could to obtain my visa. He was pretty confident. He made them believe that America is the country we all need to live and that step-by-step I would build my future. Moreover, the most important step is to have experienced the American life.

I was working that day. I had to leave, so I said bye to Mr. 'Saver' and I thanked him for coming. He put his big hands on my head and said, trying to comfort me, that one of these days we will meet in Washington to have a cup of tea and that everything will be ok then.

I waited for his call for more than two weeks. At the end, I decided to deal with the situation in another way. I had a business card from the first meeting we had with those people more the eight months ago. I decided then to send an e-mail to the office and the Academy responsible for the training and the internship, directly to the Director of Operations. I asked for some help from a friend of mine who was in the third year in the English branch of the university. I told him about my situation and that I needed a nice and provocative letter to make some people in America decide about my future. Actually the delay to get my document was related to my weak English; I couldn't convince them during two interviews we had in Casablanca. We wrote to them that I was still waiting for my I66 document (the pink form), that I passed all the exams, I had my TOEFL, and that the only way to get there is to have that form and I wished to have it in the nearest period of time. I was crossing my fingers and hoping my last chance wouldn't evaporate.

The 'big' day came when the Fed-ex van stopped next to our home. It was the first time I saw Fed-ex delivery coming to our neighborhood. I was scared something had gone wrong. I didn't want to go out and sign; I let my mother do it for me. I asked her if she could open the door and get the mail from the guy. I gave my Personal Identification Card in case they asked for it. She was also excited and suspicious; she wanted to know what was inside the package. We opened together, and there it was, the I66, the only document I was missing to get my visa.

I couldn't wait anymore, because I had everything I needed. The only thing I was missing then was a date for my appointment. I needed to go and wait again to get just a date for my interview.

After a few days, I was walking that morning next to the consulate. I went to the consulate without any appointment. I was lucky that I passed through the main door with no appointment. Someone asked me if I registered and I said I did, and then they let me in (inside the consulate). It was a beautiful, sunny and warm day in March.

My turn came and they called my number. I had to go to the window again. They asked the same questions as last time, but this time was easier. I felt relaxed; I felt it coming: the visa. I was confident. She was the lady with whom I had the interview last time. After not even three minutes, she said that I could come back in the afternoon to get my passport back. The rumors were circulating that if they keep your passport, it meant they are going to stamp a visa on it.

I called my father to tell him what happened. He was happy for me, and said he was going to call the rest of the family to tell them the good news. Later I heard that my mother was crying when she knew it because she can't bear that I will be gone in a while; I was with them all twenty four years of my life and that is going to be hard for them that I'm leaving. She said the visa for her meant that I was going to be away.

I went back around two o'clock to the consulate. I got my passport back just from the window outside. I opened it holding my breath, and there it was: the visa to go to the United States of America. I was so happy. I wanted to buy something to celebrate the event, so I went to a pastry store downtown, a very nice place. I bought a big sized cake with some ice cream for everyone in the family.

On my way back home, I felt for the first time the USA; it was so close to my eyes. And that was when I realized the weight of the decision I made to go to America.

'God bless America.'

My story summarized a chance to come to America. There are millions of stories about the reasons why people from all over the world immigrate to USA. The why and the how questions for their quests toward the American dream justify the desire to live in land of America.

Some immigrants use the legal way to go to America; my situation is an example. Others take the illegal process, due mostly to the geographic location, like the Mexicans. Let's go to America. "Vámonos, vámonos a la vida mejor, a la vida loca, to a better experience."

However, there is just one reason for those immigrants to inhabit America, the 'green bill' that makes the freedom realizable. Before the immigrants come here, they don't know if they are going to stay here one, two or more months, even years. That immigrant doesn't have any answer. He or she is just sure about one thing, the economic or social situation in their native countries and those situations are about to explode or become harder. The immigrants couldn't resist anymore. Then, the only and 'insecure' method to protect themselves and their families is leaving their homeland. They need to have a better life, and they deserve a better life. They risk those lives to go and live in the west. They are seeking to try something else, to try another country where -maybe- the possibilities and opportunities are more and easier. In certain ways, they are immigrating like any other person who is already there. They don't deserve deportation unless they break the 'right law,' a dangerous affair, not just because they come to work or live. Come *on, give me a break.* Usually when people immigrate to the

USA, they make more money, they provide themselves with a better way to live and to act with others, they integrate into the society, but in any other way they don't become more productive or smarter. Those same people in their own countries are just as productive, but they don't get what they deserve. The result is less productivity than in America. In America, they work harder but they have more compensation than being in their origin countries. They find more offers with more possibilities and more money.

Immigrants all over the world go to countries more developed than their own countries. They usually immigrate to the west, to countries such as Italy, France, Spain, USA, Netherlands, England, Saudi Arabia, even to Morocco or Mexico. There are, of course, many other countries where immigrants find a place to integrate.

They immigrate to these lands looking for a better lifestyle or in order to build a better one for their relatives in their native lands. They immigrate to Saudi Arabia from countries like Pakistan, Egypt, and Sudan…to Morocco from Senegal and Mauritania in order to have more chances to immigrate to Europe, to Italy and Spain from Morocco, Tunisia, or Algeria… to Mexico from Argentina and El-Salvador…so they can gain more spaces and reach the USA through Mexico. They try to get to the USA from the rest of the world.

CHAPTER 6
Welcome to America

I got off the plane in New York; I knew that my uncle was waiting for me outside the airport. We called him the night before and I gave him my flight number. The procedure was light and easy, not too much waiting in the airport. It was raining heavily that day. It was cloudy, cold and little windy. After, I found it wasn't that cold, but for an African like me, it was damn cold. The airport was full but seems empty. There were a lot of travelers but it seemed like no one was there. The organization of the airport took over all the busy procedures. It looked nice, new, and 'healthy.' Black, White, Brown, Indian, Asian, Arab or any other race; everyone was a foreigner and there was no difference. All of them live in the same country, America. In spite of the fact that this was my first time in the US, I already felt I was home.

I took a long walk through the hall to the immigration offices. I was looking forward to having my first contact with an American officer. People were speaking English there. My first contact was with an American authority, the immigration officer. I found out later that his job was to make the end of your trip an easy process. There I was, standing in front of him. *Come on, you made it you are in USA. I still couldn't believe it, I felt I was dreaming.*

"Hi sir, welcome to USA," he said. He was a young man between 25 and 28 years old, white, happy-looking, and nice with clean clothes (as if he just started his shift), and green eyes…he was a pure American idol.

"Hello", I replied.

"May I see your passport please?" he asked me.

I couldn't understand what he was trying to tell me. Obviously, I figured out he needed to check my passport, and then I handed him my documents. He knew I was confused and he realized I couldn't speak English. Then, the silence started getting its way to our conversation, which became more body language (at least from my part) than speaking. Obviously, nothing was wrong with my entry, and after checking my passport and other documents like the I166, he knew I was traveling for the purpose of studying, learning and absolutely to improve my English. He didn't know that all that improvement would lead me to the desire of staying in America for as long as I can.

"You're all set Sir, thank you." He gave me back all the documents, except a copy of the I166 the he needed to keep for a reference. I kept two other copies of the same document for future needs.

"Thank you, Sir." I was still standing.

"You can go now; you are ok, thank you," he said.

But, I was still standing, looking at him to make sure everything was ok.

He put his hands up showing me 'thumbs up.'

I did the same sign, 'Thumbs up.'

We smiled to each other. At that moment, I was free. I felt like I was the happiest person in the universe. I didn't get it yet, but hey man, I was already in America. Thank you God.

I didn't want to show my happiness. I didn't want to look suspicious. I didn't know why except maybe the effects of being suspicious and scared from the system, but the authorities in

Morocco still existed in my mind. We never felt secure in our countries to express ourselves. We didn't have even the freedom of being happy in public. I didn't want anyone to look at me differently in the airport. I didn't like them to think I was different or happier than the normal. I kept my self quiet. I walked around to pick up my luggage. No one talked to me or asked me anything, and I didn't talk to anyone either. I didn't know if my uncle was going to be there or not, but I had already succeeded. I was happy and satisfied. I was proud of myself more than any other time in my life.

When I was checking out in the luggage's scanner, I didn't care if they were going to find some food or any other goods. I was thinking to let them take anything they wanted, just let me go outside and breath the American wind, 'the American freedom.' And, without any idea about what was going to happen later, I was already outside. I didn't live those moments; I was spreading my wings; I was going to fly in the sky above the American soil.

I was already 'inside' America. I was in New York and god blesses it.

I saw my uncle and his daughter—an American Moroccan; they both had double citizenship. They were waiting for me outside. I never met them before here in the USA, their second country. As a matter of fact, this country is their 'native' country in some ways. They live in the US and they come to visit their other country Morocco once a year or so: summer or some other period of the year. They visit Morocco for vacation to relax and see the family and some friends. They go there to enjoy the Moroccan exotic life that they miss the rest of the year in America.

My uncle is a middle-aged father, in his forties or fifties. He is married to a Moroccan-American wife. He came to

America in the first years of the 80's. Now he got his blue passport, not because he was sponsored at his job or applied for an asylum but because of his wife. It was a smart move for them. They loved each other and he needed the papers to stay here. She couldn't get back to Morocco, so she got a job here and he got one too!! A part of the reason for their marriage was to get the papers of course, but they were in love too. They were not the same age, with the same objectives. Maybe they loved each other, but the papers might be also a part of their love. But please, with no offense, if there is a misunderstanding about that judgment, it is the problem of the immigration and not them; they were very kind during all my stay with them. It really doesn't make any difference what they have done as long as they are happy together.

I knew a friend who got married to an American girl because he said that he loved her and she loved him too. Now, he got the Green Card for ten years, and after being together for almost 3 years, he wanted to leave her by making her divorce him. At the end, she was pregnant and it wasn't part of his plans. They were planning to get back together again. Did he really mean that? The most important thing for him was the papers; he was only focused on them. They loved each other, but also the papers were a part of that love, at least for him.

Now that my uncle and his wife have two daughters, they don't feel comfortable anymore being in USA. They became more Moroccan than American. He's got a beard like a Muslim. He drives a taxi like most of the immigrants who live in New York. The taxi is one of the most reliable sources for living and saving money. Most of the taxi drivers are either from India or Pakistan.

CHAPTER 7
"Los Papeles" ... How and Why?

I never thought about the papers (los papeles in Spanish) before coming here to the US. I just wanted to be here. I only wanted to experience the American dream.

Actually, we immigrants wanted just to have more chances, more opportunities, and most of all a chance to explore our competencies, where we can have the power to decide what we would like to be or what we wouldn't like to be. However, after about three months of staying in America, it became more clear and obvious that we would love to stay in America and it was not our fault. It became clearer and more visible that we need to get American citizenship in order to do what we really wanted with our lives. It is not a necessity but a condition, a fair one to succeed, a step and an important stage to find a better job, which might qualify you as an equal citizen, an American.

Before we came to America, we just wanted to be here, but once we got here, we want more. We compare ourselves with the American people. We want to see ourselves on the same level as them. The first step is observation and the latter is application.

It is hard for an immigrant to position himself to achieve certain goals, for instance it might be impossible for an illegal alien to become for example a lawyer, a doctor or a pilot in this country regardless of the competencies he possesses. Moreover, it is absolutely worse now after the 9/11 attack.

What document does the immigrant need to prove his legal presence in America? Another reason why the immigrants are always looking for ways to get the papers is because they want to be recognized by the US government as part of the global American system. They want to be certified as subjects that exist and produce, identified physically and legally. Therefore, they can obtain the power to exercise all their duties in full freedom. In that case of recognition, they can travel to their origin countries, see their families, and come back whenever they want to America. Also, as a result, they can work wherever they would like to and they will be able to enjoy their lives more with all the benefits they will have. They can even decide to vote in presidential elections (of the country they are living in). The results of the relief this would cause immigrants in the long term would benefit the American society in some of the following ways: reducing the high level of crime, creating more jobs, building cooperation between the races and many more advantages. Adding to what have been told, we immigrants will be more comfortable paying our taxes if we were Americans, than having them deducted 'legally' from our paycheck knowing that we are illegal aliens. With the government "closing their eyes", it means that illegal immigrants choose to opt for the illegal ways to get their taxes, either by faking IDs or overstaying their visas using ultra-legal-delivered IDs from authorities. But then, if an immigrant is allowed to become a double citizen, it will be healthier for the society.

As far as I knew, to be legal in America, you need an Identification Card, Social Security Number SSN, Work permit (if you are an alien and looking for a job), Green Card or visa for Aliens, American passport, and Birth Certificate proving you were born in the USA. Is that really what you need to prove your presence in America? I'm only in possession of three pieces of identification: Identification Card, a Driver's License and a Social Security Number saying I'm not allowed to work without INS authorization. Despite this, I have been working for almost four years with no problem.

There are millions of immigrants who work in this country with no work permit, millions of them with no SSN, and millions more who don't even have any ID, any proof. The society needs them, Uncle Sam calls for their efforts. He obliges them to pay their taxes. The common point between Mexicans, Polish, Moroccans, French or any other foreigners is that they all work hard, and the Americans think about them like 'burros.'

What is the difference between a foreigner immigrating to the US to live (and work) and an American citizen working and living in a foreign country? In that case, both are considered strangers to the places are going to be. They are foreigners. However, the differences exist; a Moroccan who is working in the USA has not the same benefits as an American working in Morocco. A French or Spanish person living in the USA is not like an American living in France or Spain. The USA is the best place to work of all of them with no discussion.

CHAPTER 8
The Start of a New Life

My internship was going to start 15 days after I got to America. I spent 10 days in New York with my uncle and his family. I was a tourist there, and my first visit was to the Supreme Court (in America, you could visit any place from the most gorgeous tourist monument to the most original place like the White House). I went to visit all different attractions: parks, museums (amazing museums of arts, history, animals and science), the 'what used to be' World Trade Center (so big and high that I had to lie down on the floor in order to take pictures of that mankind monument; amazing), the United Nations (security council), the Statue of Liberty, Wall Street and many other wonderful places. During my stay in New York, I surely didn't bother myself with any kind of thought about the papers. The purpose of my trip to America was studying. I didn't think about anything else but having fun; there were no worries, no problems, and no need for solutions then. I was free and I didn't want to lose my comfort, no way.

I was just happy; every small detail in my life was filled up with satisfaction, and moreover my birthday was in a few days. I got a surprise birthday party from my uncle's family. We had a lot of fun that night. I received gifts from everyone, and I thanked them for everything they had done on my birthday.

I remember my first day in America; I was staring at

everything I saw outside the street through the window of my uncle's car. It was afternoon, around two or three o'clock. My uncle was driving the car, and I was sitting in the front. The car was nice, black, and big with clean inside and outside. We got home in about an hour. Obviously, it is not easy to find parking in New York, but my uncle who had been living there for about 18 years knew how to manage and he found parking in less than 5 minutes. We got to the building; it has several floors. There was a concierge at the doors and a front desk. My uncle went to talk to the officers there; he probably told them he had a visitor so they wouldn't bother me while I was there. We went to take the elevator to his apartment on the 26th floor. My uncle and his family live in an upper floor apartment; it is a nice, secure place with two bedrooms, a spacious living room, a hall, a kitchen and a nice view of New York's highest buildings. The Moroccan heritage was featured in the way the apartment was decorated, especially in the living room.

After we got to the apartment, he showed me everything I would need in the place: my bed, the bathroom, and the kitchen if I need to eat or drink. Then, he asked me to call my family and let them know that I arrived and I was fine. I told him, I had to take shower first and rest a bit before I call them; I was exhausted.

I put my luggage in my cousin's room: the 17-year-old daughter. Then I went for a shower; I was so tired that I needed it. The warm water felt so good, it got to every part of my body. It felt so nice and so warm that I wasn't worried about anything.

After the bath, I put on my traditional Moroccan dress and I walked to the living room when my uncle was sitting and having a cup of tea. He invited me for some, but I told him I had to pray first. He gave me a small carpet to use for praying. My uncle is a Muslim too. I have grown up with a 'modern' religious family. When I was 21 I went to Saudi Arabia for the pilgrimage. I'm supposed to pray at least five times a day which I don't do anymore, shame on me. Anyway, I prayed my late prayers that I missed while I was traveling on the plane. After I finished, I thanked god for everything and asked him to guide me in the future through what it is good for my religion and me.

My uncle told me he got a phone card we can use to call Morocco. The connection was good and we both talked to my family. We were already missing each other; they told me to take care of myself and to try my best to achieve my goals. My mother asked me not to change to a different person, to be who I am, and keep a deep faith in God and my religion; she always advise me so.

After having tea and some pastries, my uncle had to leave for work, and before he did he showed me everything I might need in case. I was by myself in the apartment, and then I turned on the television. They were some shows on TV about money, how to earn more money in some school's advertising and there were many goods publicized on TV even within the show itself. I was lying on the couch next to the window watching TV, and from time to time I was hearing sounds of ambulances and police on the street. From the high level of the window I was looking through, I could see some of the buildings downtown, and they were the highest buildings I ever saw. I was impressed. By that time it was getting dark and I couldn't resist my fatigue; I was really relaxed. I fell asleep, and the TV was still on....It was a long day.

I was sleeping like a child, deep and secure.

I didn't want to wake up. I felt so comfortable, so

satisfied and truly happy with my life with no worries and no problems.

I heard the door opening; it was my uncle's wife, such a wonderful woman. She is a typical Moroccan woman. I already remarked that all the family seems happy to be together.

I spent almost ten days with them. My uncle, a friend of his and I went to the train station in New York. My uncle gave me a ride in his car, and he even paid for the ticket. My father, his brother, asked him to do so, and he will get the money when he visits Morocco next time. It was a nice gesture from my uncle. I only brought 400 dollars with me from my country; that was all I had. The train will take me to Savannah, Georgia.

I thanked my uncle and his family for everything they have done for me to make my journey a pleasant one. I thanked them for the birthday surprise. I told them it was very nice to stay with them. Actually, they all have the legal papers to stay here, they all have the citizenship, and I'm happy for them.

CHAPTER 9
What's Coming?

Passing through seven states, the panorama was wonderful, and leaving the cold weather in New York, I found a nice and warm climate in South Carolina.

Before I was going to begin my internship in South Carolina, I already had the idea about the necessity of getting the 'American papers.' My uncle asked me the question: "Are you going to stay more than a year in the USA?" I didn't know how to answer him, but for sure, he was referring to what will be the subject for the 4 years coming starting from now: The Papers and how Mohamed is going to get the legal American papers.

By that time, when people asked me about 'los papeles' at that point, they (the papers) weren't as important to me as just focusing on starting my internship or learning that new language which is the English. I was looking for professional experiences more than American papers; I wanted to learn. The papers weren't a part of my priorities, and I didn't think about that subject and how to work for it. I didn't care; I still had my visa, and it was operating. All I had to do was to start my new life with no worries about the papers (los papeles).

Then, my reply to any question about the way to stay in America 'legally' was always opting for silence or trying to escape the question in a smart way. Anyway, I had the visa for one year, and I just spent 10 days. I still have more than 11 months to decide what will be the next step, stay or go back to my country.

It was a beautiful day of May, and by the time we were going south, it started getting warmer and sunnier.

My only preoccupation was to get to the next step, to Hilton Head Island, South Carolina. There isn't a train station at the destination I was going to; therefore the closest Amtrak station was the one in Savannah, Georgia. At that time I didn't know where all those cities are situated, and I thought Savannah was called Havana and Hilton Head Island was just a name of a hotel named Hilton. I didn't know where to go or how to get anywhere; the only effort I had done so far was to fax my train number with my name and the time I supposed to arrive in Savannah to the Academy responsible for my internship. I didn't have any idea how it was going to work, what I was going to do there, how to get there, and even why they had chosen me.

Only few years later I discovered some of the realities about living in the United States. Today, 'I've just finished my shift, and I've made 24 dollars in tips; it's not bad, plus the hours and the regular commission for the party. I work as a waiter, bartender, and banquet server. I don't even remember anymore how many jobs I have had during my four years stay in USA, and the one I have now is not bad –especially for someone in my situation. I just moved from South Carolina to Chicago, Illinois. Moreover, looking for a job in these economic conditions, issues and circumstances is not easy. Everyday, I take the blue line subway to go to work. I work with many people with no papers. Of course, they don't say it –like me I don't say it too- but it's obvious. Most of them are foreigners or Mexicans, and whenever we start talking about the papers they look interested to know what's new. We all work hard, and sometimes I feel like I'm going to collapse at work. I don't like this but my options are limited.'

Anyway, going back to that beautiful day of May, I was still taking the train that was leading me to my first step towards the American dream, to Georgia. I tried to read some magazines and newspapers and I was already feeling hungry. I opened the bag; it has chips, soda and some candies my uncle bought for me. In the store there were hundreds of kinds of chips, candies and sodas; the stores in America are full with multiple kind of products everywhere you go. I picked up some. I was hungry, starving actually, and thirsty too. After I ate, I fall asleep. I didn't want to sleep; I only wanted to get to Georgia as soon as possible. It was a long, exhausting but not boring trip. I wanted to take advantage of every moment. I enjoyed my way. I was set free. I was already in America and on my own.

In the train, there was a lady sitting next to me. She started talking to me, and she asked me where I was going and where I was from. After I told her, she was proud of and surprised about what I was doing. She told me that was a good experience in my life to visit another country. Despite my English, we were trying to communicate. She understood the situation. She was helping me to construct phrases, and she also said that her granddaughter was learning Spanish. By that time, I didn't know the importance of Spanish in USA. I didn't know it was the second language in America and that there were plenty of reasons for people to study the Spanish language. Now, I believe that the most important and reasonable reason for its emerging is the proximity of the Mexican borders and the high presence of Latinos everywhere.

I slept again. The lady left at the Philadelphia station. There was nothing to do, and moreover, I looked at all the pictures in the magazines and read all the headlines in the newspapers, so I went to sleep again. I didn't want to wake up because I was tired. I was dreaming of myself becoming someone important, somebody proud of himself, and someone who is going to do something big to this world and something that the humanity will use for the good of the universe.

From the first day of my stay in the US, every time I wake up I feel happy. That sensation of finding out that I was in America made me always feel happier than the moment I went to sleep. I remember the first time this happened to me I was in New York in my uncle's apartment. I remember I opened my eyes and saw, through the glass of the window, the high building standing and lighting up. It was one of those moments I would never forget.

I saw some people getting into the train, some taking off some cities we crossed, and some others were sleeping. They were all different types of people, foreigners for me, strangers, Americans. I didn't get used to see those specific kinds of people in Morocco. They spoke a different language than ours, a language that I still couldn't understand by that time. They dressed differently than what I used to, and they looked whiter than us. They acted a certain way we usually didn't act in my country. They speak English, and we speak Arabic. They speak English, and we -or they- speak Spanish. They speak English, and we -or they- speak French.

CHAPTER 10
5 Years in America Because of My ID

*H*ow *may days?" a co-worker asked me.*
"Ten," I replied.
"Make sure you write down all your days and hours you have worked," he said.

"I always have done it. I agree with you, you never know... thank you chef for reminding your friend," I told him.

"You're welcome," he said.

Now in my job, it happens often that the management screws up the payroll. I always need to check how many hours I worked plus how much tips I made everyday and keep track of all that. Then, at the end of the two weeks, once they give me my 'money,' I do compare between the paycheck document and the record I kept track of.

The majority of the immigrants I know work in the food and beverages business. Why not me?!!! I do too. We might ask what is the relation between 'being' an immigrant and working as a cook, waiter, bartender or even a dishwasher guy...what is the reason? I think that most of the restaurants, clubs, hotels or any other food and beverages location are hiring us regardless of our background or legal documents proving our stay in America. Moreover, immigrants work mostly just for money. They are not looking for experience or promotions, which is wrong. We need to become the elite, the best and the most experienced people in our field.

"I just need a copy of your ID and a copy of your Social Security Number." The Manager asked me.

"Ok, sir, and when can I start?" I said.

"Tomorrow, is it ok for you?" He asked.

"Here they are. This is my ID and this is my SSN." I gave him the documents.

"Ok then. I will make copies and get to you right away," he told me.

Five minutes later, he came back with the copies and the ID's and gave them back to me.

"That's it, you're all set. You can start as soon as possible, how about today?" he asked me.

"That's fine with me. I don't have any objection, and I'm ready," I said.

"Ok then, come with me." He stood up, and I followed him.

"Thank you very much sir," I said to him.

Then I had a job, a job that doesn't require any "work permit," a job that doesn't need any Green Card (or purple), a job where you don't need to be an American, or to have a citizenship and there is no need either for identification's verification nor for SSN validation or fakeness -except for some places where they check all that. Everything goes!

I came to America to have a 'true' life, a clean one, a kind of life that I already had in my country —which is going to surprise many people. It is true that a lot of immigrants in this country, including me, used to have a good life in their origin countries. Here is something to remember: I wanted to become 'somebody' in Morocco; I wasn't haunted by the idea to come to the USA. Even if there are plenty of opportunities here, to get some of them, like a good job, you need to have 'papers' to prove your eligibility that many aliens don't have, including me.

After two months in the US, some of my friends in the program advised me to go to the Social Security Office to apply for my first document that will recognize my presence in the country: the social security number SSN. *Today, I even have the EIN, an Employer Identification Number for my new 'business' I opened in South Carolina and Illinois. I bet there is no other country in the world where you can have your own business that fast.* On my way to the SS Office, I took my passport and the I66 Pink Form, the document that shows the reason I came to America (the contract of my internship). I waited for almost 10 minutes, and the officer received me at his desk. We didn't talk that much. I showed him the documents, and he didn't even ask me why I was applying for the SSN. I didn't even know why I was applying for that number. I just heard that the SSN is the first 'piece of the puzzle' everyone needs in order to accomplish his legal stay in America...I didn't know that the number in question was that important. It is very helpful in all life's needs.

After almost three weeks, I received my SSN with sign on the card writing 'valid to work only with INS authorization.' By that time, I didn't care that much regarding that sign. I was just happy to receive a document recognized from the US government. I was already 'accepted.'

After I received my SSN, it was time to get my South Carolina driver's license. The same day I went to the DMV, 'Division of Motors and Vehicles,' and I obtained the ID for 5 years validation. They said that they needed to take a picture of me to put it on my new ID.

"Are you ready?" an officer asked me.
"Wait, I need to smile," I said to her.
I smiled.

"Here you go, your ID is going to be printed in a minute," she said.

She handed it to me with a big smile.

"You have a good day, thank you".

The next step was the application for the driver's license. I failed the first time but not the second, and I had my DL for 5 years too. However, everything changed just months after the 9/11 attacks in New York and the Pentagon; the procedures got harder, and to have the ID or DL or the SSN they started to ask for more documents.

How could I work? How could I find a job with my SSN having that sign? I need to have a SSN with no sign. I was thinking of telling the SS office that I lost my number, but many people before me tried the same trick and it didn't work; they end up receiving another copy with the same number and the same sign. What can I do then?

I needed to work, and moreover I didn't need any questions about my legal stay in America, especially any proof. Some people I knew got some contacts with some Mexicans. They said it was going to cost me 50 dollars to have a fake SSN. Well, problem solved. Nevertheless, in the fake SSN there was a misspelling of my first name. I didn't want to show it to any employer; I was still worried. I asked some other guys the same favor. He was friend of mine who knew some other people, and he said that they don't like to show themselves. So I gave him the money and the information about myself, my name and my SSN, and I told him to make sure they spell my name correctly and my SSN too. After two days, those Traffickers switched me 'almost' to a legal person to work in America. I received the card and I even paid less (only $40). They said if I wanted a Green Card it would be 50 dollars extra. If someone doesn't have his or her own SSN, they provide a fake one. In my case, I already had one provided from the American Office; I just needed a fake one to avoid that 'sign' about the INS authorization. I know it was illegal, but inside me something wanted to believe that it was legal.

CHAPTER 11
Two Out of Three Goals

I still remember the first time when I arrived from New York; I got off from the train in Savannah, Georgia. It was hot, a hot day of May. The summer was almost there, and I was ready for the good time.

The people from the Academy were supposed to come for me at the station. Someone who works for the company as a van driver came up with a friend of mine that I knew from my country back home. They came on a big van to pick me up and drive me to Hilton Head Island, South Carolina. I recognized my friend, we hugged each other, and he introduced me to the person who was in charge of my transportation to our destination, Hilton Head Island, where I was going to live for 1 year during my internship. I ended up staying 2 more years illegally in that state and more years in other states, Illinois included.

Hilton Head Island was about one hour from Savannah. The van's driver was a lady, a nice American woman with a southern accent. She works for the company as both driver and manager.

We started talking for a while, and she found out that my English was poor and that I couldn't understand her anymore. Her English was so good that I couldn't follow. My friend tried to explain what she was explaining to me, but we already got bored and she didn't speak anymore. I was already tired, and I knew that I would have more of that.

She told my friend to tell me that once we got to the office I would have to meet with the manager to discuss all the details.

I thanked her for everything. Actually, I found myself lucky; not everyone came to this country and had people waiting for him in the airport or the train station, and not everyone would have a house, transportation and different other amenities to use…especially for one year.

Once we arrived, I went to the office of the Academy. I got the keys of my new apartment with my nametag and the student kit that will help me during my courses.

My friend from home helped me to carry out my luggage. I never felt as good as I did that day. I supposed this would be a nice country to stay and live in. I wasn't wrong, and the proof is that I never felt homesick. Before I came to America and when we (me and my friends in my country) talked about the US, we never knew how or what Americans were like, and we only knew that the USA has been always a powerful country which meant that its people, the American people, might be outrageous or bad people in order to 'rule the world.' But once I started living in America and being in live touch with its people, I found out that the American people are just wonderful, nice, helpful, well-educated, friendly and especially very respectful people. They helped me integrate into the society and learn the language, and I never felt racism.

Then I thanked my friend for his help. I got to my new place. It was an apartment with two bedrooms, two bathrooms, a kitchen with a table, and a living room. I started to arrange everything in my bedroom. Then, I took a shower and went to the office for the first orientation.

After we finished our meeting, there were three goals I told the manager (and even wrote). The two I still remember are:

-Improve my English.

-Get as much experience in the hotel and tourism industry as I could so I could apply it for best in my country once I got there.

Now, the third goal, I think would be to find a way to stay in America, legally.

My second goal stayed always on hold. I will be looking forward to applying and putting it to the test.

I went to my apartment. I was so tired, and I needed to sleep. I already missed my family. I wanted to tell them how happy I was, how things were going well for me, and that nothing surprised me; everything in this country was working logically, right and well-organized. That was America for me (and still is); people could stay one day or ten years, and they would always feel as free as their first day.

I told the manager all the knowledge I had in the English language and that I wanted to live with foreign interns. I knew there were many of them from the same country as I. I did want to communicate in English with my roommates and learn from my mistakes rather than communicate with the same language I have been using for more than 20 years.

I was in South Carolina so I could learn how to experiment and improve my professional skills. I could have done it anywhere else, but I have chosen America because of the language and the economic-social leadership of this country in the world.

When I lived in my country, I learned methods and courses of action totally different from those in this country. I have been working in various establishments: banks, hotels, travel agencies, airports, and even with a political party. It's hard to compare 'third world country' procedures with a country on the level of America. In addition, I wanted to observe and learn how things work in the 'first country in the world' and even experiment with them under my own mode….Wouldn't that be interesting? Of course, it would be.

3417 was the apartment number where I was living during the first year of my 'American dream.' I will never forget that number, and from then it has been my lucky number. Before, I never had any apartment on my own in my whole life. I never had my own place to live; I always used to live with my family, and it was their house.

At the end, I felt like somebody, someone who counted, who built a big part of his life with effort and work. I deserved that interest because I worked for it. I already felt useful in my new life. I had the chance to meet people from all over the world and from all continents: Africa, Europe, Asia, America (South & North) and Australia.

Before I went to sleep, I called my family to tell them I arrived, and that all was ok. My father was the one who picked up the phone this time. He was by himself at home. We talked for a while, and when everyone came home, they called me back; I was happy and satisfied to speak to them. I also called both my grandparents and one of my friends. By the way, all my friends were pissed off because I didn't tell any of them I was coming to America. I don't know why I did that, but I was sure that was the right thing to do; maybe it was because I was a little bit of a believer in bad eyes and I wasn't confident in any of them. I didn't want any force -human or supernatural- to take me away from my trip to USA. I succeeded. I was going to sleep at the end because I was so tired.

The dream started, it was different that time, a bad dream. I dreamed of myself trying hard, really hard, with all the power I had to get a big quantity of hair out of my throat. It was there. I felt it. I felt the sum of the hair, and I tried hard and I still try because that dream is still with me. I couldn't get it off off my mind and from my throat. It was a lot of hair mixing inside my mouth, and I could barely breathe. Although I was sleeping, I could still feel it. My fingers got inside my mouth. They were touching a part of it and trying to get that heavy mixed hair out of my stomach, but I couldn't and I still can't get it out today. It stayed inside me, in my mouth, in my stomach, and even in my brain. Why? Why? Why? All frustrated, I woke up. I took a shower, and I went to the Jacuzzi inside the building where I live.

My roommates were from other countries; one was from Turkey and the other was from Colorado, US. I shared my room with the Turkish guy because that room was bigger than the other one. The American intern was always making noises. One of his hobbies was playing guitar, and he also liked to play golf. Actually, golf was the main activity and sport of the Island (Hilton Head Island), and most of the tourists visited the island for the main purpose of golf. Later I found out that Hilton Head Island was one of the richest places in the South. Obviously, the American Dream was pictured on every place within the States, and Hilton Head Island was one of the best locations for the golf lovers.

It is very clear how to find a way to be happy, no matter what you are going to accomplish or not. Anyone who breathes in the USA is fully or partly satisfied in life's sides.

Be proud to be an American, or just be proud to be in America. I am not an American, but we were proud to be in America. If 'Osama Bin Laden' was in my situation, he would be proud to be in the USA. He would be happy to see the Niagara Falls, or go for a trip to the Smoky Mountains, or visiting

CNN in Atlanta, and he would be looking forward to having the American Express credit card in his wallet. But, he would never have thought about destroying other innocent people' dreams. Thus, he deserved to be away from this world.

We love the world through you, and we love the world by way of every place and every mankind respecting the growth of peace actions.

CHAPTER 12
No Time for Love

When I was in New York, I never called her. Once I got to South Carolina, I tried to talk to her twice by phone, but the connection wasn't good enough to make the calls. She was in England studying her career; she went to a school in London.

We first met in a private school we went to together in Casablanca. Her name was Leila. She used to be my classmate, and she was a very nice girl. We spent the first year just as friends, and then we got together. My parents knew her, and she used to come to my place to study together. The two families even met each other on many occasions like graduation for example.

She went to England to finish her studies, and from that time we tried to keep in touch. The first and the second year were perfect, and then during my third year in America things got different. We didn't talk to each other for many months.

However, it was harder than we thought to stay without calling each other. I remember just a few days after I came to New York, I called her, but by that time, she didn't know I was in America; she was surprised. Actually, she wasn't that excited about it. She didn't show a lot of enthusiasm about it. By that time, I felt something was wrong. I thought that she was seeing someone, but I didn't have any reason to believe so. She was calling my family regularly and sending me pictures of her, letters and all kind of contacts. I gave her my new phone number; we talked from time to time. We called each other, and when I don't find her I just leave her messages, and she always called back. I was trying to call her often, knowing that I'm not good at calling people, but I tried with her. It was different. Sometimes, when I used to stop calling her for a while, I used to try to justify the reason I didn't call her because I don't usually call people, even my parents only in emergencies or when there is something important I would want them to know, she said that she was not my parents but my lover, my girlfriend and she has the right to hear my voice anytime she missed me.

In my country, we had a good time together. We shared so many beautiful souvenirs. She is an optimistic girl, and that's what I liked most about her. For instance, whenever she used to leave me messages on my cell phone, I felt her smile through her words. I like girls with vivacity; she was one of those kinds.

Suddenly, after a few months in the USA, she was wondering about our relationship, and she said that it would be a mistake if we keep our love. We just needed to forget about 'us.' She justified her decision by the distance that kept us away, and that we were only dating from school; for her it wasn't a serious relationship. She didn't believe that our relationship was going anywhere. We hung up the phone, and we weren't together anymore. She still had my phone number, and I told her to call me anytime she wanted to talk.

After that call, we talked like two or three times before she said one time that she wanted to apologize about what she said and that she didn't know why she said that. She told me that she loves me and she will love me forever. I didn't know what to tell her by that time, but two months later I forgave her and we got back together.

I didn't want those affectionate problems to influence my internship. I didn't even bother myself too much. I was relieved from any decision I could make. I started my internship, and I was really proud of everything I had done.

'Integration,' this is what every alien needs to improve by living in the US. It doesn't matter where you come from, what you speak or how long you are staying. Anyone who is coming to this country has to integrate into the society. It isn't necessary for us as aliens to become Americans in culture, but we need to *create a link* between our world (where we came from) and the American world.

I was trying to integrate; I was trying not only to learn a new language but also to apply and use it. In addition I was learning new habits, how people react, how they manage their life, and how they get in the line to get their needs. I especially attempted to absorb how American people live in their houses. My roommate was an American subject, which was definitely integration.

To integrate in this country, you are required to be born in it; April 15, 2000 was my birthday in this country. I was born again; my 'second' life began when I was 24–years-old. I was born again with no family and no American birth certificate.

CHAPTER 13
Do You Speak English?

A month and half later, I was already starting my new and second job in the program. It was a Sunday evening. I usually had my days off during that time. I used to work on the weekdays and sometimes weekends in other resorts. I liked my job. I used to be activities organizer by the pool for guests spending their time on the island. I was Activities Director, entertainer for all the tourists and the kids in the hotel or club where they stayed.

A month earlier, I worked in the kitchen. It was my first experience in the USA and my first one in a restaurant. It was a fine dining. However 70% of the people who worked in the kitchen were Mexicans or South Americans. Because of my skin color and my accent, they thought I was Latino too. I felt that during all my stay in America. The first language they used to communicate with me wherever I went was Spanish; I'm not Spanish, I'm an Arab-African-Muslim. Anyway, I learned many skills from the month I spent in the kitchen. The American chef was very talented. He was the last one to show up in the kitchen, and the first one to leave it. They take advantage of their professional skills, those chefs, Assholes. He told me after if I stayed with him for one year I would be a chef too. I didn't care about that. It was hard and not worth it to spend more time there. Two reasons made me leave that job: I got allergies on my hands from the heat, and my English wasn't good enough to understand what they were telling me. I was working in the 'line,' the hottest and most important part of the kitchen. I even went to a hospital and got some medicine to cure my skin; my hands were burned.

Lack of language and health conditions took me away from my first job in the country. The second reason (health) might be treatable, but the first one was, in contrast, hard to fix. What possibly could be done?

I needed to have more close friends able to speak English as their native language. I needed to get more friendly with interns speaking either no other language than English or some of the languages that I don't speak so I wouldn't have any choices but English. In addition, I needed to watch as much television as I could with the caption switch 'on.' Therefore I had watched movies repeatedly with and without the caption option on. I used to see movies twice or three times to get used to the English vocabulary.

In the program, we had seminars twice a week. They were similar to small classes for discussions and researches about our supervisory program and training for two hours each session. Most of the time, I don't get to participate because of my English level. Although I was always present, my attendance didn't serve either the teacher or me well. The results weren't so good.

I needed another solution; I needed someone to be with all the time. I wanted an English speaking girlfriend. I also wanted love and sex by the way. However I never wanted or thought to have an American girlfriend or to get married because of the papers. I just wanted to speak with people in English.

She wasn't so beautiful but she was very sociable, very nice and most of all friendly, so I could even know and meet more and more people. I met my new girlfriend and she spoke

English. Her name was Sarah; she was from South Africa, a good English-speaker. I didn't plan to be with her just for those reasons. She always used to say that she was the 'best,' and I always smiled and still smile when I think about that. I also liked her, and we stayed together for the rest of our internship.

To be part of the American society, you have to speak their language. To get the papers (los papeles) or the citizenship, you need to pass many tests and one of them consists of a 'quiz' about the American history, the states that form the USA, the presidents of the US...and some other questions about that land we want to stay in.

In order to have a chance to get the American papers, you need at least to speak the language. To succeed in whatever you are doing in that country, a good skill of communication is very essential...and Mexicans, Chinese, French or whatever people come to the USA need and have to speak English as a part of their success. Otherwise they might spend years and decades working in descent jobs; meanwhile others like Irish, Australian, or even Arabs who speak perfect English might achieve their goals in a short time.

Thousands or even millions of foreigners stay strangers in America because of many reasons including the color of their skin, the look, the habits, the traditions, the religion, the language and other personal motifs linked directly to each individual are all reasons curable and treatable in some ways. Those strangers always stay in the middle of two worlds, their native countries where they came from and America where they live and work now. They become a person with no identity. If those Mexicans, for instance, don't often integrate the American society it is because of that lack or trouble of identity. The look is also an important factor; it is a part of the immigrant integration. It is hard to look like an American and it is impossible, for instance, to change the color of your skin or your eyes. Thus immigrants need to choose between their identity and the west one.

Why do we, foreigners or aliens, all get frightened and worried when a police officer pulls our cars over? In California, for example, the INS with the police always interfere and arrive when there is a fight in a nightclub. There might be deportation directly from the club to back home (Mexico, Morocco, wherever) for the immigrant. Being worried is a part of our lives as people without legal papers in America, with or without reason.

To live 'correctly' abroad, in other country than yours, you have got to be a part of the country you are traveling to and you have got to integrate. In order to do it correctly, you must get papers, ID cards, vote and other citizen rights.

Before coming to the USA, there are plenty of tips to learn for immigrants from countries in Africa, Europe, Asia or even south of America. America has a different image of habits and traditions than any other country; it is a world full of various and new tips. However, if you were a Portuguese going to live in Italy, there is no big deal in differences between the two countries' cultures. A Moroccan who never watched baseball or American football before needs more than a year to understand that game, and for a Spanish from 'Spain,' it would be more less the same story for him to learn the rules of playing baseball or American football. The same Portuguese wouldn't need those kinds of experience to go and live in Italy; they don't play baseball but they play soccer, which they do also in Portugal.

We, aliens, all need time to integrate. We are all in the need of time to get the papers. 'Los papeles' are not supposed to be easy to get, and that was why I was always against the lottery strategy. Life in this country is different than any other, and giving them the papers with no effort was and still is a big mistake.

CHAPTER 14
Kiss the Green Card

My internship was in progress, and three months passed when I received a call from my family. Actually I talked to them almost twice every week. This time they were calling me to ask about what I was going to do. They asked me when I was coming back to Morocco and if I was coming. I replayed, "I don't know, but probably next year after I finished my internship unless life brings something unexpected."

Actually life didn't, but the interns did. It was absolutely clear for them to stay in the USA. Life was much better for them and it was going to get better. After four or five months, however, I started to wonder what my decision was going to be. Was I going back before my visa expired? Or was I staying and ignoring the law, the American law?

I had to decide. I needed to know how was going to end up my decision. Was it going to be positive or negative? I didn't know at that time.

Today I realize that I planned this: I planned to go back to my country but only when I wanted to, not when a paper (visa) on my passport said so.

My first year in the USA was planned as a year to improve my English and get me the certificate from the Academy. My second was to get to know more about the country, relax, have more free time and especially have a good and fun time. The third year I concentrated on hard work, saving some money, improving my skills, getting more experience and applying some of what I learned during my first two years. My fourth year was to study and get new skills in various areas within the USA. The fifth and last year was to try to get my papers, and if I couldn't get them then I would go back to my country.

My decision was to stay in America for at least 5 years. However, I loved traveling, so it wouldn't hurt me to leave this country. I didn't decide it in one day or one month...as a matter of fact, I never knew when I might decide to leave the country, because it was not up to me: The immigration authorities could deport me anytime, or something big could happen back home (death of a relative for instance), then I would have to go back. I wasn't too explicit about my decision to anyone else because, and this is what every illegal immigrant does, you don't trust anyone else.

I liked the life I lived at that time. I had a job as 'activities director.' It was a lot of fun, and people usually enjoyed being around me. I made their vacation more fun with more entertainment and especially more activities.

I had a J1 visa, which meant one job and no other income than the one in the contract. It was worse because on my social security card, it said 'not allowed to work without INS authorization.' All of the other Moroccan interns had second jobs, why not me? More income, more experience, more contacts...and moreover working in the Hyatt hotel, which was going to be more fun. I was going to work; no experience needed. I worked as a waiter helper for 10 dollars an hour cash, with no social security needed. All they needed was black shoes and black pants. Transportation, a bow tie, and a white tuxedo were provided. They even filed our taxes and I didn't know how they did that.

In the US, they have a very essential tool, credit cards. Credit cards are tools full of money, money that you don't physically have but you could use. I went to the closest mall in the city; I was looking for something to buy for my family. With my second job I was already saving a lot of money, 1500 dollars that I was going to spend on some gifts for my whole family. It cost me almost 1500, everything plus the fees to mail by plane. Within those expenses, I spent almost 400 dollars in banana republic, and it was the first time, not the last one, that I applied for a credit card. I was denied. Plus, just for reference, every immigrant sends money to the country he or she belongs to. We all send money to our families and relatives. It doesn't matter if you denied that, it would be always on your shoulders. In my case, I would never transfer money to my country; I believe in getting rich by individual sacrifice and whenever you split your cake you will never get satisfied. If everyone gets a part of the cake, no one will be rich. As a consequence, I'm not rich because I send money to my country. And if I do everyone could.

However, today, after almost 4 years, I own two American Express cards, one unlimited, and a Visa card, one MasterCard and a Discover card with a 5000 dollar limit.

In the USA, the system is built up to make it easy for you to apply and obtain different kind of cards going from grocery stores' discount cards and passing through all types of Credit Cards till, maybe, the Green Card. Nevertheless we don't get that in Morocco, absolutely not in Mexico and not even in Jack Chirac's country. That was one of the reasons that made up my mind about spending more time in that land of USA. It was all was related to a place linked to an advanced technology country.

Immigrants in this country, America, are making more money than in their native countries. Most of them live better lives, have bigger houses, nice cars, and expensive clothes; every part of those accomplishments came from what they believe in. They live the American dream. The papers shouldn't be a very important goal. If they enjoy their time in the US, they wouldn't care about the papers. Being in America illegally is not supposed to be a crime, but being a terrorist (Osama Bin Laden's companions) is illegal.

We, illegal immigrants, don't care about getting the papers or not. There are two reasons for aliens to apply for residency: the desire of visiting our family and the wish for looking for a better job in the USA as an FBI agent, CIA....

In our countries we all dream of America. Everyone wants to come and visit America. We all know that it is a lot of fun to be in Disneyland or to visit New York, Hollywood, Miami or Las Vegas. We all wanted to be looking, watching and being in those cities and the reasons that build that desire was what we always heard about this country through the television, radio, cinema, and propaganda or even from people who visited the land of freedom.

It was not our fault that we wanted to live in this country, but the human being habits and the desire of improving our quality of life guided us. It was not the American's own responsibility or fault to collect all nationalities; USA was built that way, it is a country of immigrants. It was the time of the technology and plus every civilization in history went through that kind of immigration of people. In the past people who were looking for wisdom or trade traveled wherever they had to in order to look for their quests; the Romans didn't ask those people for Green Cards.

The world was a place for every humans being, and I wouldn't accept someone to throw me away from a land that didn't belong to any particular person. I would be free to live wherever my feet could take me.

CHAPTER 15
A Year in America: No Worries

Weeks and months passed quickly and my English started to improve. I even used to give speeches every Tuesday morning to the guests from the reception next to the pool in the residence I worked for. It was a very expensive location called 'The Island Club.' I loved it when I used to work there; people trusted on me, they were very nice and I made good money. I used to work only in the mornings on weekdays. In the afternoon, if I don´t go to work at my second job (cash), I used either to go to the beach, or to play tennis, or choose to go and swim in one of the three swimming pools located at the resort, or to walk into the Mall, or to bike, or just to watch television by myself or with some friends; there was always something to do. Once every month the Academy used to organize social parties outside, and all the interns participated and used to enjoy the evenings with drinks, food and multiple activities.

I remember the first one (social party) I went to was a cruise to see dolphins for an evening. It was my first excursion after just a month in the USA. The best was coming, more excursions, parties of all kind, and trips to Orlando, Miami, Colombia (capital of South Carolina), Charleston, Atlanta, the Smoky Mountains, Jacksonville, Savannah (during Saint Patrick's day for instance), and many other wonderful places.

All kinds of fun everyone is missing in our countries back home, you find it here in US.

I met interns and people from all over the world, and they all love this country. However some of them don't show that love but I could see and see it on them. I knew people from France, England, Germany, Portugal, Japan, South Korea, Hong Kong, the Philippines, Poland, Italy, Czechoslovakia, Russia, Morocco, Egypt, Lebanon, Syria, South Africa, Zaire, Kenya, Nigeria, India, Afghanistan, Pakistan, Canada, Mexico, Argentina, Australia, Switzerland, Hungary, Malta, Spain, Ireland; those are most of the countries I knew people from, and I learned from their behaviors and the way they live that anyone from anywhere in the world would love to live and stay in America. I'm sure that they would enjoy having the Green Card in their wallets. There is no exception for other countries not mentioned. Nowadays, every human being needs to possess the papers from every country not only the American ones, they make your life much easier.

The first year of my life in the US was a combination between starting to think about the 'papers,' learning English, meeting people from all around the world, working in different places such as restaurants, four different pools in various residences, Hyatt Hotel, Hilton, The Marriott, having sex more than any other year of my previous life, learning supervisory skills in Tourism and Hotel Management, getting my South Carolina ID cards and the SSN, opening an American bank account, and especially getting ready to live and specifically depend on myself.

The second year was more challenging, but nothing was planned by that time. I knew I had an uncle in New York and I could live with him, but I wanted to depend on myself. I had the option of staying another year in South Carolina with some friends. What did I do then? After weeks of thinking about it, at the end I decided to stay; I ended up by staying two more years in South Carolina before I moved to Chicago, Illinois –accompanied by the best 'gift' god ever gave me in the USA. It was the first time I felt happy for my choice of something different than just thinking about how to get the legal 'papers', having somebody to share my life with was my new priority. In addition to the four years, I spent my fifth and last year in Las Vegas, Nevada.

On Hilton Head Island, I had to work almost everywhere with fake or no papers. Most of the employers used to pay me cash. They don't declare me to the IRS, so they don't pay taxes and on the other side they don't ask me for legal papers to work. Fake papers meant a fake Social Security card (or SS Number) that cost between 40 and 60 dollars and fake IDs or Green Cards that cost between 50 and 60 dollars. A special deal of SSN and Green Card could be bought for 100 dollars. Most of the Mexicans know all about those maneuvers. They are more likely to have contact with some of the fake IDs dealers.

In my case, I already had a legal Social Security Card before but it had the sign that shown the obligation for the INS authorization to be delivered separately if I wanted to work in the US. The fake one didn't have any sign. It was with the same number I had, and thus it counted as an American Social Security. I used my name and the right Number the Social Security Administration office provided me to obtain a fake document. Therefore, those Mexicans helped me in some ways to find a job without legal documents, and it stayed that way during all five years of my stay in America. Without them, I wouldn't have been able to continue my life in the States, and it stayed that way during all the time I spent in South Carolina, Illinois and Nevada. I used to always hear about illegal immigrants (that I knew) resisting the stress of not having papers and working everywhere in the US from the east coast to the west coast.

CHAPTER 16
More Years, More Worries -In America-

I already knew I was staying in South Carolina for my second year. The girlfriend I used to date left the country to go to South Africa, but when she came back there was nothing between us. We were done with our romance that never got farther than the internship. Thanks Sarah for everything. She was really a nice girl, but when it comes to life's steps it is not important to be a nice person. I needed to move on. On the other side of the world, there was still that Moroccan girl I would never forget, Leila, still living in England, and slightly in contact with each other. We were fighting the distance that kept us away, and whenever we missed each other either we would talk on the phone or we send letters. She used to call me more than I called her, and one time when she was in Morocco, she left a message saying that it was very urgent to call her. I called her and she said that it was absolutely important to tell my parents about our future and that we had to get married or at least get engaged. I was shocked, and surprised. I told her that we weren't ready; I didn't think she was ready and most importantly I wasn't ready. By that time she got mad and justified that through her parent's pressure. I thought she knew what she was doing, but once she went back to England she called me again to say that she was sorry and that she shouldn't have acted like that, and that I was right. I didn't feel comfortable. I didn't usually like people to rush me or rush things around me. I was in America, she was in another country, and our families lived in a third one. How could we work our ways out? We didn't have our own house, and there was no solid career for me, no fortune made yet; we were building our future step by step. However, the only worry for her was about our age. She always used to say that we were getting older. The truth was that I was older than her but I didn't care; I never cared about the age. Anyway, things didn't work for us, but we kept in touch for a longer time. Despite all that, I would never forget that we had good time together in Morocco. She was still virgin (which was normal in my country). We used to have special sex. She was petite, and I used to take her in my arms and we just kissed each other.

She stayed in touch with me more than I did with her; she has been calling my family many times (I liked that). My mother used always to ask me about her. One time I called her mother and she was very happy. They were a nice people to me, and I loved that.

I wished everyone good luck. Things didn't work between the two of us, but who knows what the future will bring. If I had the US papers, maybe it would be different...the papers play a major rule.

After I was done with my internship, I was already in possession of many letters of recommendations, certificates, diplomat as a Tourism and Hotel Supervisory and lots of experience plus absolute satisfaction from my managers on the way I handled my internship. During the last weeks of my contract, we were already looking for an apartment. I was definitely sure I wasn't going back to my country after my visa expired. We found an apartment of two bedrooms for 750 dollars, me and two other Moroccan friends —one from the south and the other from the north side of the country where we come from. Then, by the time I finished my contract with the Academy (the Exchange Visitors Program) we already moved to the new apartment. It was a very beautiful place and a nice neighborhood.

As I had a long year of transition from the life in my country and the new one in the USA, I wanted to have some vacation to put everything in order in my mind. I took a month long vacation with no work and no big feeling. I already was putting some money in savings, about 3500 dollars. I was just relaxing, reading books, watching TV, hanging out with friends, going to the pool; I felt satisfied.

A month later, I was already looking for a job. I started first a part time job with a catering company –the same one I used to work with during my internship as a second job. They used to provide me with transportation (that was very important for someone in my situation with no car). My two other roommates used to have good jobs, they both worked in restaurants, one was a cook and the other was a server's helper.

They both had a regular income. I just used to sleep, drink, go to parties and use the internet in my spare time; sometimes I played tennis or went swimming inside the complex.

My balance in the bank was going lower and lower. Two times I couldn't even pay my rent, and my roommates always waited for me to pay them -late. I never wanted my balance to go below the minimum required, and sometimes I asked one of my roommates to loan me some money.

I was looking for a serious job, a job that would pay me monthly, weekly or daily, just to pay my bills. I called many places, and I always used to read the employment section in the newspapers. The major problem was that if I found a job I would need a car to go to that job, which I didn't have. I started looking for more shifts with the catering company that provides transportation.

I even tried to apply for a truck driver's position. The only issue was about the contract; I had to sign a 5-year contract. I showed the instructor in the truck company my real Social Security card, but he didn't care about the sign and he said that he would be willing to hire me; I just needed to sign the agreement. I could make between 900 to 1200 dollars a week, but I didn't want to be doing the same routine driving day and nights for 5 years. I didn't want to sign for a big part of my life in America doing the driving business. And moreover, I was worried about my legal situation in case I would have an accident. The importance of the 'papers' always occurred. To cover my charges I was also working as floor woodcrafts person, I used to install wood in some villas floor, bedrooms, and halls.

I needed a solution. It arrived from one of my roommates (the guy from the north). Obviously he didn't have papers (he came to USA as tourist and he stayed), so he asked me if I could do him a favor by putting a *car* he was going to buy under my name. His work was almost one hour from where we used to live, and there was no other method of public transportation. Because he couldn't ask people anymore for a ride to and from work, he decided to buy a car, but the problem for him was that he didn't have the South Carolina IDs to register the car under his name. The papers worked on my side that time, because to get the license in the DMV he needed the South Carolina Driver's License, and the only document he got so far was the ID from Florida. That was it; at the end I had a car.

He paid for it, and I was the driver. I used to give him a ride to work and keep the car for daily needs and leisure. I could start then looking seriously for a job. One month after we bought the *car,* I had already started my new job; I was working in the kitchen as a dishwasher-boy at a French restaurant. I didn't care if it wasn't a nice job —I respect any kind of job where you could make money legally. I made up to 500 dollars in two weeks. That wasn't at all bad as a start, and meanwhile I was looking for another job. After some weeks I was promoted; they moved me from the dishwasher service to the pastry side then a line cook.

Months passed and I found a new job, a good rewarding job. My English was already good enough to get me a better job; I started a new job as a waiter. One of the experiences I like about that job was that I had to take a boat to get to the work place. It was located on another island, about 30 minutes by ferry. "Haig Point" was a residential golf club situated in a small island called "Daufuskie Island" in South Carolina. It was a private club; to get there you need either to have membership or to be a guest of a member. I used to take the boat from Hilton Head Island to access Haig Point through the ferry to Daufuskie.

Haig Point was a residence for almost 250 members, very rich and famous people. Most of them were retired; they live and stay in a community playing golf and having fun.

There was a Welcome Center and two Golf Course, one with 18 holes and another with 9 holes, a Clubhouse, a Beach Club, a Mansion, a Lighthouse, a Valet for the luggage, two Swimming Pools, three Tennis Courts, hundreds of nice houses (for the members), a Cricket field and many other amenities that make life in the club more and more enjoyable.

I used to work in the Clubhouse, in the food and beverage department, for more than a year. There were four restaurants. I really enjoyed working there; the majority of the members were very friendly, the weather was always wonderful, the people I worked with were professional and helpful too. Sometimes we had some complaints from the members, but we always knew how to handle them.

During Christmas time, some members decorated, by themselves, the restaurants and the entire Clubhouse; they felt like home. "Haig Point" is truly a wonderful place to live, and to work.

One day, I heard that the INS was in the Club. I wasn't working that day, but the next day all illegal workers (Mexicans, Argentineans and others) who work there in landscaping or construction didn't show up. I didn't know what happened, but once I knew about it I was really worried and I started to be more suspicious. I started watching everyone's step –on the boat, in the club, actually everywhere. Some of my co-workers asked me if I was ok concerning my 'papers' situation. I told them (I always used to say that) that I had the 'work permit.' I actually never knew what that document looked like. I always used to say to the co-workers I work with that I was resident of the US and that I had the legal papers to stay in America. If they were foreigners, they usually said the same thing, but with the majority of foreigners rare were those with legal papers to stay in the States.

I got my job just after the 9/11 attacks in New York and the Pentagon. Some people asked if it was easy for me to live in place where they are 'scared' of Muslims. All the time, in the Club where I worked, I used my real name 'Mohamed.' I think that those people who attempted those actions within the American soil did it actually against every human being, and whoever supported that were not human beings. I'm not only a Moroccan African, I'm also a human being. Americans, Europeans, Asians, and all nationalities must find a way to work together. Those 'killers' were Muslims, but it wasn't an excuse for their acts. Christians, Arabs, Indians, or Jews might do that too. They have done that not because they were Muslims, or because they were illegal aliens with expired visas. They did those 'terrorists' attacks because they had problems; they didn't love life, they had hatred in their hearts, they were not brave enough to fight their issues, and they had chose the easiest way to show the bad side of any human being. What they did anyone else could have done it: not only Muslims or Arabs, which was why I kept using my name anywhere I went in my job and life. I love life.

We need to love human beings with their advantages. We need to love people from anywhere, Muslims, Judaists, Buddhists, Christians, and any with no or other beliefs. We don't have to judge. We are all people in the world and I just want peace.

CHAPTER 17
Next Step: Bye America

I made some good money at the 'golf club' job, and after a year and half I paid all my debt, sent money to some of my friends and family, opened new 'small business,' bought a car, possessed many credit cards, succeeded in saving more than 18,000 dollars and most important of all getting ready for the big move to Chicago, Illinois. I was more ready to move to a big city than two years ago.

These were considered as two good years to prepare myself. The gift I mentioned earlier that god gave me was a girl I met; her name was Rosa.

The first time we met was in a Moroccan party and I remember perfectly that night. It was in November 2001, and after we had some wine and good Moroccan foods they asked me to give speech. I thanked the guests for coming; they were Americans, French, Spanish and Moroccans. Then, after the party was finished, everyone wanted to go to nightclub. We went out and came back home late that night. After everyone left I asked Rosa if she wanted to spend some time with me and she accepted. I didn't plan anything. Everything came by itself and we were happy.

We made love the same first night. She was unique, meanwhile we were on bed making love she started crying. It was bizarre for me. I didn't know why but I was already in love with her from that night and I told her that I loved her in the first night. Later in our relationship, I asked her about that night and why she was crying, she never told me why.

From that night, everything was different; we had a different relationship from any that I'd ever had. Our love and life story was inexplicable but lovely and full of excitement and warm affection with some tiny and spicy disagreements, some up and some down. I felt more comfortable with her than any other girl; I always felt at 'home' and safe with her.

She used to be my neighbor in South Carolina, and then she moved to Chicago one year before I did and lived together. Because she wasn't an American, she used to go regularly to her country for Christmas and summer holidays. The only time she didn't go for Christmas was the year we were living together in Chicago. We fought to stay together, and we did it; we went together to Chicago and lived in the same apartment close to downtown. We went to many places together, to Niagara Falls, to the Smoky Mountains, to Atlanta, to Charleston, to Las Vegas, even to Rushmore, New York and California. You never really believed I loved you Rosa. The truth was that I did, I do and I will. The only issue was that we were always looking for the best way to do things, which was hard to accomplish!!!

Maybe the next step would be Spain, a new 'birth-land.' *Let's see…*I was ready. Rosa was actually from Spain. Was it about the 'papers' again?

It wasn't the case! What happened? What did Mohamed do? Where is he now?

Only two weeks after I moved to Chicago I started a new job in a hotel in downtown Chicago. It was a famous place for businessmen to meet. Few months later, there were some serious rumors about the INS getting to the place where I worked in Chicago, and then I decided to do something I would never have done without deep thinking. I wanted to get married to my girlfriend; at least I would get the Spanish 'papers', and finally take away all the pressure of a probable deportation back home. The Food and Beverages Manager was a friend of mine. He told me that some agents from the Immigration office came to ask about me at work. He said that they had a call from someone who told them about my situation in America. Till today, I never knew who did it.

Anyway, I didn't tell my girlfriend what happened. I just told her that I didn't like to work there anymore, because 'I don't make enough money.' One week later, I left my job with no notice; I told them I was leaving the country. I asked Rosa if she wanted to marry me in her classroom at school. It was a surprise for her. I didn't tell her I was coming to visit her at school, and I just showed up at her class when she was teaching the kids and I asked her to marry me. She was exited and happy, and then she told me that was the happiest day for her. We went to the Chicago downtown's county to get married. We were in love, and I didn't want to leave her. After two months, I went by myself to Las Vegas, Nevada. My wife couldn't come with me because her contract with the Spanish program was limited to some cities in America other than Las Vegas.

I worked in a hotel, and they didn't ask me for 'papers' at all. I met a Moroccan guy over there. He helped me to find that job, and he was a chef in a big hotel. That Moroccan guy was my 'other' uncle I had in America, who I hadn't talked to for more than ten years. In Las Vegas, we used to go to parties together. He was about 50 years old, a big guy with long hair and very strong body.

He used to live by himself, so I moved in with him. We used to drink and go out every night. Las Vegas was a good city to have fun and do millions of things everyday.

The year expired and I had to live the country. My wife

came to visit me that summer in Las Vegas. And things were different than before, our relationship was going through many problems, most of them related to her wanting to go back to Spain to live there, her work contract was about to expire. With limited options, I didn't want to go with her, so I decided to go back to my country. I left America, and we met just one time after that. We met in Morocco because she wanted to divorce; she was staying in a hotel, without even seeing my family. She said that is the best solution for us to finish our relationship, because she said-I wasn't living with her in Spain. She decided to marry a Spanish guy who was a teacher. But for me, I didn't care. I didn't want to divorce her. I just stayed in Morocco, and I didn't do anything at all. Everything was almost done for me.

I remember I was getting off the plane in the Casablanca airport. My family and some of my old friends were there. They were happy to see me, however I thought none of them was looking at the person they said bye to more than five years ago. I was a different person. After just two weeks of my stay, they wanted me to marry the girl I knew, the one who used to live in England. They didn't know I was already married with the Spanish teacher. The reason why I couldn't tell them was because she was not Muslim. They would never accept her as my wife. It was summer time in Morocco, and I had the chance to meet my old girlfriend, Leila, she came to visit her family on that summer. I managed to find her phone number so I could call her. Few days later, we met over a breakfast at her place, and then we went for a walk by the beach. I asked her if she got the papers for England and she did. I didn't ask how, but she did. She doesn't have any engagement or boyfriend that will keep us away from each other. Therefore, our parents planned everything for us. No matter what happened they just wanted us to get married.

Anyway, we got married, and we lived together for a while before deciding to go to England. This time it was me who didn't want to go. I already had no job and I had an addiction for marijuana. I smoked a lot, and the doctor told me if I don't stop I would die in three or four months. I didn't care what he was telling me. I was always smoking that drug because I wanted to remember those days in America.

I still remember them. However, I'm not going to stop smoking, I'm not going to divorce the Spanish teacher, and I'm not going to England to live with my Moroccan wife. I'm just staying in my country because I believe that Morocco is my birth-land country, and it will be the place where I'm going to die.

Today, I lost everything.

I wish my family knew that I used to drink. I never told them about it. They asked me before but I denied it. They asked me actually if I smoked too, and I didn't tell them the truth. I always wanted to tell them what I do. It didn't matter for me. But there I was lying about things that I did. I just wanted them to know the person I was, no lies no problems, just who I was, who I actually am. America was the reason for some of the rules I broke; I got more freedom than I was supposed to have...

EPILOGUE

This book is, as I was thinking before I started working on it, my story in America, from my memory.

I needed to tell you that I was in the United States of America, that this country is the best country of the world, and that I never regretted any minute I spent living there. God bless America.

I'm Muslim because I was born in an Islamic country; you are catholic because you were born in America. Then, why we have to hate each other if we don't even decide about our beliefs? I think that most of the extremists, either in the Muslim world or any other religious trend, don't even like their own people, their own origin. They have been denying and ignoring the laws, their families, their countries, and worst their religion; and that's how people like Osama Ben Laden live their lives.

A month before I came back to my country, I tried to do something big, something that my soul would be grateful for it. I didn't want to do something different from the usual to prove myself, I didn't want to destroy, and I didn't want to be a terrorist to be famous. I never liked the way Muslims behaved toward Christians. We need to love, not to hate. I didn't want to bomb any place, and I definitely didn't want to kill anybody to become famous. The news media would be looking for someone with a name like mine to justify our tendencies, but that wasn't me. Sorry, but not me. What I tried to do a month before was to write and publish this book. Why? Because the

American people need to know that not every Arab is a bad person, and that not every alien is bad. I hope I succeeded.

I'm Muslim, and my name is Mohamed. Those facts about me would never weaken either my soul or my origins or my beliefs.

Let's be together and not against each other. When I was in America, the first book I read –and have till now- was the Constitution of the United States of America; I needed to learn the law that govern the country so I could fellow it during my stay.

To my idols

About the Book

For more information or to receive a free review copy, please contact the author at alien.arab.inamerica@earthlink. net. Alien...Arab...and Maybe Illegal in America is available for sale online at Amazon.com, Borders.com, BookSurge. com, and through additional wholesale and retail channels worldwide.

About the Author

Mohamed Fandi was born in Morocco and studied law in Casablanca, his city of birth. A descendant of Berbers and the son of a very conservative Arab family, Fandi came to the United States and eventually graduated with honors in the field of Tourism and Hospitality Management. Mr. Fandi and his family now reside in Chicago, Illinois.

www.ingramcontent.com/pod-product-compliance
Lightning Source LLC
Chambersburg PA
CBHW060413290526
45791CB00002B/725